BEHIND LOCKED DOORS

HUMAN WAREHOUSE: 1950 Insane Asylum

AND

MEMOIR OF A MAN'S REGISTERED NURSE TRAINING

ROBERT J HIGGINS

Additional publications by Robert J. Higgins:

ROAST BEEF IN APRIL
Robert J. Higgins
ISBN 0-9637936-2-4

MIXED FEELINGS IN VERSE
Joan Higgins
ISBN 0-9724551-0-8

Copyright © 2013 Robert J Higgins

All rights reserved. For information contact:

excorpus1@yahoo.com

Climbing Rose Press
87 Theresa Boulevard
Binghamton, NY 13901

ISBN:1491289988
ISBN 13:9781491289983

Library of Congress: 2013915158
CreateSpace Independent Publishing Platform
North Charleston, South Carolina

Cover and editing advisor: Cassandra Higgins
Front Cover: Wagner Hall, Binghamton State Hospital
Back Cover: Main Building, Binghamton State Hospital

Available from Amazon.com, CreateSpace.com and Other Retailers

*I dedicate this book with love
to my dear wife, Joan,
and
my sons, Bob, Randy, Stephen, and Kevin.*

FORWARD:

A remarkable and insightful look at education and conditions in mental institutions during a period of time when we all thought *life was good*...after World War II. How sheltered most people were from the realities of life on that "Hill" where reality for some didn't exist. History, as played out in Bob's vivid descriptions of daily life in the mental institution, is not something we learn about in school or hear about on Facebook. One has to wonder, after reading about the horrors of patients' lives, if we didn't ignore it *all* because we couldn't change it or because it was all too horrific to think about.

Willow L. Garney

Retired Teacher
1961 - 1992

INTRODUCTION

Behind Locked Doors serves a dual purpose. The first is to acquaint the reader with a broad description of the three-year diploma for nursing education in the early 1950s. More than fifty years have passed since nursing education left the hospital setting and came under the collegiate umbrella in an effort to upgrade nursing's professional standing.

Second, the book is also directed toward creating an awareness about the care of the mentally ill in one New York state hospital, though all hospitals were essentially similar in the care provided. Prior to 1960, there were no active treatments or medications to treat mental illness. In-hospital care for the psychotic was primarily directed toward psychotherapy, maintaining order, and protecting the patient.

In today's world, it is hard to imagine a hospital setting aimed at protecting the patient from harming himself until the passage of time and occasional psychotherapy provided a remission of symptoms and a hopeful discharge to a useful life. Too often these modalities resulted in expected failure and filled mental institutions.

This book provides one person's view of the three-year nursing program as it was in 1950 and a historical insight into mental health care from a unique student's viewpoint. The care of female patients is not discussed because there were legal and social barriers to male nurses caring for women in the 1950s.

CONTENTS

Introduction	1
Contents	3
The Beginning	5
Closing the Past's Door	27
Binghamton State Hospital	29
Psychiatric Commitment in the 1950s	35
Medical and Nursing Staff	39
Binghamton State Hospital Nursing Program	45
First Autopsy	47
Fairmont	51
Broadmoor	57
Electric Shock Therapy	67
Insulin Shock Therapy	75
Lobotomy	79
Hydrotherapy	83
Psychopharmacy	87
Surgery and Central Supply	89
Ward 6	99
Main Building	105
North Building	111
Bellevue: Opening Another Door	117
Senior Year	149
Reflections	159

THE BEGINNING

It was a beautiful, sunny September day when Pop and Willie West drove me up the state hospital hill to Ferris Hall. The approach to "the Hill" seemed like that of an attractive college campus, with mature trees, expansive lawns, and old, weathered brick buildings. Missing were the young students lounging around the buildings or going to classes. Instead, I saw groups of men and women shuffling behind a person wearing a white jacket and followed by another employee. The groups were dressed in drab, unpressed clothes; some were in oversized denim coveralls. Further along, nurses in starched white uniforms beneath black capes with red linings walked with men in white outfits. In another area, groups of men were raking leaves or mowing grass with rotary push mowers, frequently stopping to make gestures and speaking to unseen persons.

I had second thoughts about entering this nursing program. What was I getting into? Though the weather was fine, my fear of the unknown darkened the day. I wondered if this place was a concentration camp, prison, or madhouse, as perceived by the average person in Binghamton or in the movies. Nevertheless, I pushed my fear into the background, put on the young man's bravado, and acted eager to plunge ahead into the educational adventure.

While traveling from our home on Liberty Street to the Hill, a distance of just a few miles, my mind wandered back to what had brought me to enter a nursing program. Who ever heard of men in nursing? What would people think about a man who identifies himself as a nurse?

While playing two-handed pinochle one day at our home at the Jungle Club Bar, my graduate nurse neighbor, Pat, suggested nursing to me as a method to finance medical school. Her reasoning made a lot of sense: complete the nursing program at the state hospital and use the nursing income to finance my ultimate medical school education. Financing education was a formidable barrier. I had declined a track and wrestling scholarship to Hartwick College in Oneonta, New York, because I could not foresee how I could provide the cash for room and board. The state hospital nursing program would pay me thirty dollars a month, included free room and board, and required no tuition. All I had to buy were the books and uniforms. It was the answer I needed to get out of the minimum wage rut and get on with my education. To hell with those who might think of me as "limp-wristed." I was on my way!

Willie and I had planned to enter nursing and share the unknown together. His goal was to become an RN and be a psychiatric nurse at the state hospital. His dad and brother were attendants there. He was going to go one better because a registered nurse at the state hospital enjoyed an elevated status. When we decided to enter nursing, Willie was living at my home for the past six months. Because of family problems, Willie had been living with his grandparents. Farm chores and basketball practice collided, and the grandparents threw Willie out, telling him to never come back. Willie was among my best buddies, so he came home with me until he found a place to live. Pop liked Willie and invited him to live with us until the school year was over. There was one big proviso, however. He had to assume his share of the work around the bar, the Jungle Club.

However, when the school year was over, Willie got a wild idea and decided to link up with a couple of guys and hitchhike across the country, doing farm work and earning money to enter nursing in September. He did that and made it across the country and back—though with two problems: Willie returned with no money and was too late to enter the freshman class with me.

Our parting at Ferris Hall was a sad moment. It was heartbreaking for Willie because I knew how desperately Willie wanted the education. Although he was assured entrance to the next nursing class, he had initially applied to become an attendant. Since there were no vacancies, he enlisted in the navy for a three-year term rather than waiting to be drafted into the army for the mandatory two-year military service all young men faced at that time.

As for Pop, my deliverance to the state hospital to enter the nursing program was a happy moment: his son was going beyond a high school education. I remember well his unforgettable admonition when I was a teenager: "You'll finish high school, goddammit, or I'll break your neck." Now I was going beyond that, and Pop was thrilled!

Pop reminded me to come home when I could since home was about a fifteen-minute bus ride. He gave my shoulder a shake and wished me well with a broad smile around the ever-present unlit cigar. I couldn't help but notice that his eyes were very wet. That was an intense moment of expression for Pop, who had much difficulty conveying tender feelings. At that moment, there was a lot I could and should have said to Pop to thank him for the moral guidance and living principles he instilled in me, but I didn't. With a few words, like yep and OK, I turned and entered Ferris Hall with Willie helping me carry my stuff to my room and began my new life.

Ferris Hall

THE BEGINNING

I surveyed my new world. It was a first-floor room, about ten feet by twelve feet, and had a small closet. The bed was made of iron rails, flat springs, and a three-inch mattress stuffed with something that had lost its resilience years ago. Later, I found out that the stuffing was horsehair. The dresser was a four-drawer antique with a large mirror with serious aging defects. Two of the drawers had barrel locks with no key, and a small desk was under the window. The window was the best part of the room. It overlooked a nice expanse of lawn that connected to the street. I had brought my own bedside table—a wooden orange crate.

Secondary to my Grundig all-band table radio, the next important item that I unpacked was my Big Ben alarm clock with pie tin to set it on. I had a terrible time waking in the morning, and I needed the amplified noise of the already loud Big Ben.

I discovered that Ferris Hall was home for many attendants and was divided in half to separate the sexes. There was one bathroom for each section with a half dozen showers, toilets, and sinks. The toilets were flushed by pulling a chain attached to a water reservoir about six feet overhead. Flushing was indeed loud and effective.

The community snack bar and store was beneath a large auditorium about thirty yards beyond the Ferris Hall side door. Here, one could buy sandwiches and snacks, stationery, and replacement uniforms. Employees, visitors, and patient trustees frequented it. Except for uniforms, one could hardly identify a patient from a visitor or employee out of uniform. Of course, the tip-offs would be a patient trustee engaging in a conversation with an invisible person or the keys dangling from an employee's belt.

Assembly Hall

By evening, all my male classmates had arrived. There were ten men in a class of thirty, and I was the youngest at eighteen. The rest were all ex-GIs in their early to midtwenties. Early on, I had some difficulty relating to them outside the classroom as an inexperienced kid just out of high school. That would eventually evolve into a close camaraderie, yet our lives off the Hill remained private save for the good times at John's Bar, which was located close to the Court Street entrance.

In the early months of the program, one of the classmates stood out starkly. He was well over six feet and had a weightlifter's physique that had been developed while a hod carrier prior to school admission. He also had a very likeable personality and the amazing ability to drink an eight-ounce glass of beer in one gulp. Unfortunately, he had to leave school within the year because of an ever-increasing varicose ulcer with complications that would not respond to treatment. Another classmate had to leave during the first year due to active cavitating pulmonary tuberculosis. He was admitted to the downtown tuberculosis sanitarium, later had successful lung surgery, and ultimately became a certified professional accountant.

Two other classmates had known each other before entering school. They remained good friends throughout training, forming their own clique of two. It seemed that their main goals, beyond studies, were chasing the female classmates and partying.

The days following were a confusing jumble of books, uniforms, introductions, and learning my way around the hospital. The big incentives for entering nursing at Binghamton State Hospital were that room and board were included and that there was a stipend of thirty dollars per month. The thirty dollars bought uniform replacement items, additional books, and cigarettes, and I was free to spend the rest with carefree abandon. I quickly discovered that there wasn't enough money for cigarettes to last the whole month. That problem was solved by buying extra long, unfiltered Pall Mall cigarettes and cutting them in half with a razor blade.

The uniforms were the most unusual clothes that I had ever put on. After issue, they had to be sent to the laundry. Upon return, they were so stiff from the starch that I had to shove my arm down the pant legs to make way for my legs. I was quite a sight in the starched pants and surgical shirt that buttoned up the side of the chest and up the neck. Finishing the uniform was the starched white jacket and white buck shoes. Laundry was frequently returned with rips and buttons crushed. It became an inside joke that the laundry had special button crushing and shirt ripping machines.

My female classmates had it really tough. Their basic dress was a short-sleeved mattress stripe pattern that buttoned and had removable studs. The starched white collar was attached separately. Finally, a starched apron was attached with studs. An equally starched bib would later be attached after the probationary (probie) period. It must have taken the girls ten to fifteen minutes just to get dressed in the morning.

THE BEGINNING

For the first few weeks, we were subjected to the usual curriculum of anatomy, physiology, pharmacology, and, of course, nursing arts. Nursing arts meant learning to do all the things that nurses do to care for the sick in body and mind. A featured participant in the nursing arts class was Mrs. Chase. Mrs. Chase was a full-sized practice dummy on which we practiced by going through the simulations of nursing procedures. The instructors emphasized the mitered corner when making a hospital bed. It had to be almost perfect. Much of the nursing class work was fun and easy. However, there was a downside: dealing with all the orifices of the human machine, few of which are pleasant to behold, especially in the sick.

During the probie period, the class was taken to Wagner Hall for our first contact with patients. We were to practice making beds, this time with a real person in the bed. Off the class marched to Wagner Hall. The teacher gave us no indication about what we were to expect. As we entered the building, the overwhelming odor of stale urine, feces, spoiled food, and Lysol disinfectant hit us like a brick wall. Some of the female classmates had to go back outdoors, but being a farm boy, I was familiar with many of the odors and adjusted to the smell quickly. My big anxiety was about what I was going to see that created these odors.

The female classmates were separated from us to go to a female ward while the men were led into the open men's ward, which contained at least forty patients.

Wagner Hall

The beds were not separated from each other by screens or partitions. The only furniture was an enameled, simple, open bedside table wedged beside each bed. Almost all the beds were low and without side rails. The absent side rails must have been a quiet acknowledgement that, if the patient somehow fell out of bed, it might not cause great injury. Other factors were the space requirements of the rails and the cost of providing them. The mattresses were about four inches thick, enclosed in a plastic bag, and without inner springs. The bedsprings were the flat, interlocked springs such as that used in my own room and were hardly conducive to comfort and good skin care.

The noise was deafening to me. It seemed that every patient was yelling, moaning, or groaning. Some were grasping at open air, kicking, or trying to get out of bed. As I was led through the ward, patients alternately were just staring, calling us, or completely ignoring us. Almost all were elderly. When we finally arrived at the nurse's station, we were given a background description of the purpose of the ward and the type of patient on the ward. It was a custodial ward, so the patients had end-stage degenerative diseases or had experienced severe strokes. Most were psychotic or uncommunicative from their disease processes. I was sure that if a patient weren't psychotic when he arrived, he would be in a short time from being helpless in that chaotic, stinking mess twenty-four hours a day, week after week, with almost no change in the auditory or visual environment. Family visitations were few and far between, the patient having been gradually left behind in the progress of his or her family's world. Wagner Hall was a sort of staging point or waiting station on the way to the cemetery. The patient's primary contact with the world was mealtime, bed change, and position changing time. Beyond that, the patient was ignored and allowed to drift into a dull consciousness that became worse each day.

It is easy to condemn the attendants for a lack of concern for the patients. However, one must consider that there were possibly only four attendants and one RN to care for the forty and more patients on most days. It was a full day to just feed, wash, and care for these patients with little time left to establish any kind of rapport with them, if communication was even possible. I'm sure that working Ward 73 day after day was a mind-numbing experience.

I was the unlucky one of my ten classmates. I drew a bed with a patient paralyzed on his right side. He was incoherent, combative, and incontinent. When my teammate turned the patient on his side, avoiding the attempts at the biting, the swings of his good arm, and the yelling of what must have been curses, I was greeted with a bed full of feces, soft and sticky. The instructor came over and guided me in the proper method of cleanup. She was wearing a long-sleeved, French-cuffed white uniform, and I noted that she didn't volunteer to demonstrate the process. Somehow, I cleaned up the bed, changed the sheets, and even washed his buttocks and testicles, which had dangled in the fecal mess. I received a satisfactory check-off on the procedure.

Little did I know that much of my nursing experience would entail jobs best suited for farm overalls rather than my starched white uniform, but there was nowhere to go but up after that experience.

Later on in the nursing arts class, we would venture out again to Wagner Hall to demonstrate the skills learned. I even became adjusted to the smells and yells of Wagner Hall and the bedlam that enveloped the building, making them seem normal. This included bed baths, enemas, mouth care, urinary catheterizations, and other basic nursing skills.

It seemed that I seldom drew a cooperative patient for the demonstrations at Wagner Hall. For instance, my demonstration of a soap suds enema administration was on another incontinent, combative patient. When I finally was able to position the patient, insert the rectal tube, and begin the flow of a liter of fluid (liquid soap in water), the water simply leaked all over the bed. The instructor was satisfied with the setup and technique, leaving me to clean the patient, who was covered with a soapy fecal mess from his chest to his knees. Upon leaving the building,

THE BEGINNING

the instructor was critical of my appearance because I had water and fecal stains on my uniform. She condescendingly allowed me time to change uniforms.

During our first six months of training, we were referred to as probies. We were on probation and could be asked to leave on nearly a moment's notice. Refusal to perform a nursing procedure because it was repulsive or if there were attitude problems were both good reasons to be given walking papers. During the last few days of that six-month probie period, each student was called to individually meet with a panel comprised of the school's trustees and faculty. With the exception of one male nurse instructor, the rest were women, for a total of about a dozen persons. They sat in a near semicircle with the student in the middle. It reminded me of the Catholic Inquisition. The head of the school conducted the meeting in which the student's record was reviewed, as well as the student's attitude and demeanor.

I watched some girls come out of the meeting crying, though most were merely somber. I wondered what was in store for me as I wiped a smudge off my white bucks and smoothed my starched shirt and jacket. I had remained standing after putting on the fresh uniform to avoid creasing my pants.

Would I be asked to leave?

Would they commend me or condemn me?

The nursing school was rigid in attitude, almost militaristic. The instructors were expected to be treated as superiors, with deference to their ranks, which demanded unquestioned obedience. Maintenance of near-perfect personal appearance was demanded of all students at all times. This did not fit with my ingrained attitudes. I chafed at the humbleness required—and it showed on a number of occasions. However, looking back at the strictness, it did mold and smooth the rough edges of my independent attitude and made me a better person.

Sure enough, my grudging submission to the expectations of a couple of teachers almost caused my dismissal. My above-average marks were my saving grace. I was given a sort of conditional approval and walked out of the meeting grateful for the near miss. The overall result of the evaluations was that one student was asked to leave because of poor grades.

It seemed that the final hurdle to remaining in school was the draft, a two-year military commitment. I was the only one of my male classmates to be eligible for the draft. At age eighteen, I was classified as 1A, the top of the pool of eligible draftees. With the Korean War was ramping up, the odds were good that I might be drafted. As might be expected, the call from the draft board soon arrived, and I was to report to Syracuse for induction. I took the notice to the nursing office and shared my concern, and the head of the school made a phone call to a friend on the draft board. Within a week, I received notice of reclassification from 1A to 2A, which was an occupational deferment essential to the local war effort, thus avoiding the requirement for annual review for the duration of the war. I really benefited

THE BEGINNING

from the old saying, "It's not what you know but who you know."

The capping ceremony heralded the official end of the probie period. This was the acknowledgement of successful completion of the six-month probationary period and full entrance into the nursing program. During the candle-carrying ceremony, conducted in the auditorium above the community store, the probies came forward to receive the insignia, showing full acceptance into the nursing program. The girls received the plain nursing caps, and the men received the Maltese Cross patch, which was to be sewn onto our jackets. In addition, the girls were given the privilege of adding the starched bib to the apron and wearing the black nursing cape. Following the usual prayers, acknowledgements, and speeches, the class recited the Florence Nightingale pledge:

> I solemnly pledge myself before God and presence of this assembly
> to pass my life in purity and to practice my profession faithfully.
> I will abstain from whatever is deleterious and mischievous
> and will not take or knowingly administer any harmful drug.
> I will do all in my power to maintain and elevate the standard of my profession and will hold in confidence all personal matters committed to my keeping and

family affairs coming to my knowledge in the practice of my calling.

With loyalty will I endeavor to aid the physician in his work and devote myself to the welfare of those committed to my care.

Progression through the probie period meant that I was qualified to be assigned to a nursing unit in one of the hospital's buildings. When I received my assignment, I had to go to the fire station to receive a key to the ward that I was assigned to. This key was huge, about three inches long, and looked like a gigantic skeleton key. A heavy key chain that was about two feet long was a mandatory purchase. Ward keys were never detached from the uniform for fear of having them taken by a patient. Along with the key chain, the theft of a teaspoon from the dining room was necessary. The spoon was bent into a tightly compressed S shape. The handle of the spoon clipped tightly over the belt, and the key ring clipped onto the upright end of the spoon. The bent spoon key holder was a kind of unspoken, necessary part of the uniform worn by nearly all the male employees and was a quiet way to blend with the other men. Purchasing a store-bought belt clip for the keys would have been unthinkable.

The feeling that I had arrived was punctuated by being given the choice of eating meals in the employee dining room in the assigned building or eating in the North building as usual. Most of my classmates and I chose to continue dining at the North building because the food was

THE BEGINNING

generously served family style, and it gave us a chance to commiserate on common problems. In addition, the North building was close to the Ferris Hall residence.

Now that the probie period had ended and I felt secure in the nursing program, my daily activity settled into a routine of rising at 6:00 a.m., going to breakfast, and walking to my assigned ward. I always walked to the assigned building which was usually a great way to start the day. Whatever the weather, the walk to work was a time to reflect, appreciate the campus beauty, and just enjoy being alive. The assignment was usually a medical ward rather than a custodial ward. After reporting to the head nurse, I might be assigned to bedside care, assisting with patient showers, or mingling with the ambulatory patients.

My first assignment was again to Wagner Hall. I was to report by 7:00 a.m. and begin the ward routine with the attendants. The first chore was the rush to change linens on all the patients before breakfast, cleaning the incontinent patients first. With more than forty patients to change and get ready for breakfast and frequently less than five workers, there was no time to exchange even small talk with the patients.

Breakfast was an unforgettable event. Each patient was given a white bowl full of lukewarm oatmeal that was splashed with milk. A peeled, hard-boiled egg was plopped into the middle with a dry piece of toast on the edge. The toast was allowed to slowly become soaked with milk. Feeding this disgusting meal to many of the patients was most difficult. Either they could not swallow well and the oatmeal would simply dribble out of their mouths, or they were not interested in eating. This frequently meant dodging swinging arms and food being spit at you. It was years before I could enjoy oatmeal or a hard-boiled egg again. I don't know why aprons weren't issued to keep uniforms clean because I always came away with body fluid stains or food caked on my uniform. Each day as I left Wagner Hall to enjoy the fresh air during the walk to class, I would pray that none of my family would ever be in a position to be admitted to such a hellish place.

In the 1950s, there were no nursing homes as we know them today. If an elderly person became unable to care for himself or herself or could not receive continual care from a family member, the person could be cared for in a private home that catered to the elderly disabled. Such care was frequently too costly for the average family and very few beds were available. With few available beds and limited resources, families turned to the family practitioner to assist in securing admission to a state hospital. The family doctor, with the reciprocal agreement of a colleague, would certify the person as incompetent and secure admission to the hospital. This admission became a life sentence to an ambulatory ward or Wagner Hall at the state hospital.

Following ward duty at seven, it was time to report for classes at 10:00 a.m. in a uniform as fresh as one first put on at the start of the day, including the white buck shoes. It always seemed that I had to hurry back to Ferris Hall to change my uniform, or I would face severe criticism and a notation in my file for a dirty uniform. It seemed that each instructor carried a notepad to immediately jot down the most minor infraction. A description of the nursing program as being as rigid as military basic training would be accurate. After a break for lunch, it would be two more hours of class, followed by another two hours at my assigned ward.

Hanging around the community store, drinking ten-cent coffee, and playing Ping-Pong or pool in the back of the store occupied my early evenings. That was followed by the bookwork. Wednesdays were the day bread was baked at the hospital bakery. A good friend, related by marriage, was a baker there. He would give us a couple of loaves of freshly baked bread to eat while we studied. Anticipating the bread, one of the guys would bring a pound of butter from the classroom kitchen. We'd primitively tear off a chunk of bread, spread the butter with a tongue depressor, and enjoy bread that has never been equaled since for pure, good flavor.

Later in the year, all my male classmates would be rotated to surgery. Seventy percent (140 proof) ethyl alcohol was always present in gallon containers for sterilizing instruments that could not be autoclaved, that is, sterilized under steam pressure. The assigned classmate would fill an eight-ounce bottle of the alcohol and bring it to our rooms. Another classmate would remove a quart of juice from Hecox Hall, the main nursing school kitchen, so we could mix our own cocktails. After a couple of the potent cocktails, studying usually ended and evolved into wide-ranging discussions.

Fridays and Saturdays, we were free to leave the campus and go into Binghamton, but we were required to be back by midnight. Female classmates had to sign in and out at their Hecox Hall dorm and were supervised by a live-in housemother. The men were on their honor in Ferris Hall to abide by the curfew, but we seldom did. The girls chafed at this, even though they realized that the men were ex-GIs, except for one man (me), and needed no supervision or protection. The hospital, however, had an obligation to parents to protect their daughters because all but two were less than twenty-one.

Hecox Hall

THE BEGINNING

I usually went home via a fifteen-minute bus ride and visited with Mom and Pop for a little while. Just before entering the nursing school, Mom and Pop sold their restaurant, the Jungle Club, in a suburb east of Binghamton. The business had not been going well and was sold at a near loss. This financial distress forced them to move to Liberty Street, a poorly maintained, lower-middle-class neighborhood in Binghamton. They lived in a two-bedroom walkup apartment. Their previous home, while far from fancy, was spacious and bright and was attached to the restaurant. This downward move must have been a hard emotional shock, akin to turning back the clock and living the Depression again. When I entered the rooms, I was struck by the overall drabness of the apartment. It had not seen paint in many years, and the drabness was offset only by the color Mom brought into it with our furniture. The fixtures and appliances obviously dated to the 1930s and were in poor repair. The back door opened onto a tiny porch (landing) that was in such poor repair that I had second thoughts about its safety.

Mom was in good health and still worked at the Endicott Johnson shoe factory next to Calvin Coolidge School on Robinson Street. Pop, however, was having a terrible time getting work. It seemed that no one was hiring, a chronic problem in Binghamton, unless one had a trade that was in demand. Pop had none. To make matters worse, Pop was in poor health. He was a solid thirty pounds overweight, a moderate asthmatic, and alcohol-dependent. Though they didn't say so, I knew that Mom and Pop wanted me to stay home and watch television on the twelve-inch black-and-white set with them and give them some companionship, but I just didn't want to remain in that dreary apartment. In a short time, I found reasons to return to the hospital, and I now deeply regret that in retrospect.

Weekends were a time to have fun. That meant walking or bumming a ride to the bottom of the Hill to Court Street and dropping into John's Bar for a few ten-cent beers, watching the Friday night fights on television, and just passing the time. When there was a group of us, we'd toss money onto the booth to create a kitty to pay for the beer rounds. By midnight, I had spent the one dollar that my budget allowed, had more than my share of beer from the kitty, and needed to find a way back up the hill to Ferris Hall to begin another week of the same routine. I seldom went to the movies because I lacked funds, and there was no television in the Ferris Hall foyer or the community store. Even if television were available, I was not interested in watching an unending parade of cartoons and documentaries on the only channel available. There was always pool and Ping-Pong in the store and a lot of reading. Occasionally I'd play tennis if I could find an opponent with an extra racquet. When I struck out looking for diversions, I could, heaven forbid, return to my room and study.

CLOSING THE PAST'S DOOR

Entering nursing school meant a nearly complete lifestyle change. My closest buddies became shadow people. Willie had enlisted in the navy after failing to be admitted to the nursing school. Ronnie and Gerry, my high school buddies, went to work for a supermarket. It was as if a door had closed on my past. A new door had opened, and involvement in nursing and Binghamton State Hospital became my new life. On a few occasions, however, Ronnie and Gerry would arrive at my door in Ferris Hall with a six-pack of beer. Their evening visits were infrequent and less often because illogical fears of mental illness made them anxious. Our worlds were separating.

During the first year, Ronnie and I would travel the back roads looking for abandoned cars. Somehow, we were frequently able to talk the owner into giving the junk car to us or selling it for a pittance if we would take it away. Then we would go the junkyard and sell the car. The junkyard would do the pickup, and Ronnie and I would split the money. Eventually, of course, we became bored with searching for junk cars, and I had saved enough money to buy a car of my own. One of the male head nurses had a 1932 Model A Ford sedan rusting in his garage, and he sold it to me as is for thirty dollars. Ronnie helped me tow it to a back corner of the parking lot behind Ferris Hall so I could work on it. For just a few bucks, I had it running and ready for the road. It completely solved my transportation problem. I drove that nearly twenty-year-old Model A with almost no mechanical problems until it was time for me to go to Bellevue in September 1951. And I sold it for seventy-five dollars!

BINGHAMTON STATE HOSPITAL

The Main Building ("the castle") sat atop a hill overlooking Binghamton, New York, and was the nucleus of the hospital. It was designed by famed architect Isaac Perry in 1859. Described as a Gothic-style castle, the building was constructed of heavy gray stone with turrets and ramparts and looked like a foreboding castle from a B horror movie. The interior had beautifully ornate woodwork, stained glass, sweeping stairways, and ceilings more than twelve feet high. Initially the site was privately built as a treatment center for alcoholism. Later, the state assumed ownership with the official name being New York State Inebriate Asylum. In 1879, the asylum was dissolved and converted to an insane asylum.

Main Building (Castle)

During its peak use until the 1960s, the main building housed the administrative offices, the pharmacy, and a few private rooms for special trustee patients. The post office, barbershop, outpatient clinic, surgical operating rooms, and Wards 5 and 6 were frame additions facing the assembly hall, which connected to the rear of the main building.

By 1950, Binghamton State Hospital housed up to three thousand patients within a two-hundred-acre campus and was spread out among a number of old, weathered buildings occupying the high ground on Binghamton's east side. In addition, the hospital operated large dairy and vegetable farms at Five Mile Point and Colesville, which were managed by long-term trustee patients. Many of these patients were eligible for discharge but had no home or family and remained as permanent residents. It was a good solution for both parties: the hospital had laborers to work the farm, and the patients had free room and board in a secure environment.

At its peak, the hospital had grown with individual buildings arranged behind the main building in a campus-like setting. They had such obvious names, such as North, South, East, and West as well as Wagner Hall, Broadmoor, Fairmont, Hecox Hall, Ferris Hall, and Woodlawn. In addition to the patient buildings, there were the necessary security and fire, laundry, and laboratory buildings, and even a building to make slippers and patient clothing. The Ferris Hall and Woodlawn buildings were available for employee and student housing. The assembly hall and community store were located in the area that became the activity center of the campus. Arrayed about the expansive grounds on the north side of the main building were the resident psychiatrists' homes. They increased in quality until the director's home, a mansion also designed by Isaac Perry and built in the late 1800s.

Nearly every building that housed patients had at least one ward that cared for chronically ill, ambulatory psychiatric patients, and patients needing bedside care. A few nursing units included ambulatory patients regressing to a vegetative state, brittle epileptics, and failed prefrontal lobotomy patients. Much of the patient population, however, consisted of long-term psychotic patients who had failed the perfunctory efforts at treatment and were being warehoused in one of the back wards. The ward selection was based on the degree of psychiatric disability.

Garvin Building

In early 1950, construction of the Garvin building began. The huge building could house nearly a thousand patients and administrative offices. It opened in the middle of the decade and was state-of-the-art for psychiatric care. It featured terrazzo floors, steel doors, huge dayrooms, and bed wards. The windows avoided the characteristic heavy wire mesh covering and instead had extra-sturdy, small awning windows. Upon completion in the late 1950s, the Garvin building became the focus of care for the hospital's patients, drawing patients from the outlying buildings and contributing to the ultimate decline and emptying of those outbuildings. The introduction of psychoactive drugs that allowed early discharge to home and community and the depletion of the census by aging and death resulted in a severe reduction of the inpatient census. The supporting patient buildings on the farms five miles away closed.

Today, the main building is empty but avoided the state's desired destruction through intense public interest in its preservation. It is fenced to keep the curious away and is awaiting renovation with tax money. Except for the Garvin building, all the buildings are emptied of patients, being torn down or simply closed, and allowed to deteriorate. Driving through the campus today reveals the depressing sight of rusting, crumbling, and boarded buildings. One can see the foundations of previous buildings and guess where other buildings stood. Overlaying this negative vision is the campus itself. There seems to be an almost deliberate lack of campus maintenance, with overgrowing weeds, volunteer trees, and crumbling pavement. The property bears little resemblance to its attractive park-like appearance of the 1950s. Even the remaining Garvin building shows a severe lack of care. Only a very small portion of the Garvin building is occupied by the mentally ill. A portion has been leased to the Veterans Administration for an outpatient center, and the SUNY medical school leases another section. The bulk of the remainder of the building is empty, excluding the special service sections, such as surgery, x-ray, and dietary.

PSYCHIATRIC COMMITMENT IN THE 1950S

VOLUNTARY ADMISSION

A person presenting himself for admission still required certification by two doctors before being confined to the hospital. Voluntary admission extended for sixty days and would lead to a legal hearing. Results of the hearing would determine the end of the voluntary admission and discharge or indefinite, involuntary commitment.

With the exception of the commission of a crime while mentally ill, the reason for admission against a person's free will was to protect the patient from himself and others. In most cases, the routine for commitment was for the patient's benefit and safety. Persons with less than altruistic motives could subvert this process.

Usually the admission was a near emergency, where there was a fear that the patient would harm himself or herself or others. The police would deliver the person to the hospital for a fifteen-day admission using written certification by two doctors who were not necessarily psychiatrists. During this fifteen-day period, patients would be placed in a locked ward and would be interviewed by a psychiatrist, a psychologist, and a social worker. Near the end of the temporary admission, the patient would be granted the required legal hearing within the hospital or would be taken to court, where they could attempt to convince the judge of their sanity versus the psychiatrist's opinion. A person could have a lawyer if they could afford one, but the courts in the 1950s weren't required to provide legal advice. If the patient was well oriented and only mildly impaired, he could frequently win release. Yet the presence of a lawyer and family support would make a huge difference in whether the patient won release and could try to pick up the pieces of his life or was involuntarily committed for a sixty-day period. Losing sixty days in one's life could be disastrous, from losing a job and home to a total wreckage of a life. Without the interest of a loved one or a lawyer, more than a few normal persons disappeared into the back wards.

CLOTHESLINE CASE

An example of this was a young man who was admitted from the Broome County jail for threatening his wife after accusing her of having an affair. The man was very emotional and aggressive toward his wife and anyone who intervened. So the police transported him to Binghamton State Hospital for the involuntary fifteen-day observation period.

The patient claimed that his wife was being unfaithful to him after he went to work. He said she used apparel on the clothesline to signal the husband's departure and indicate that it was safe to visit. This assertion and his aggressive manner, while he insisted he was sane, caused the psychiatrist to place a tentative diagnosis of paranoid schizophrenia.

As part of the social work evaluation, a home visit was made. The wife, when interviewed, denied any extramarital affair and the use of the clothesline as any kind of signal. On subsequent visits to observe the home, the social worker noted that when certain items of feminine clothing were hanging alone on the clothesline, a man would enter the home. Upon confronting the wife with this information, she admitted the affair and the signals.

The husband was counseled regarding anger management and subsequently discharged to restore his life. This case illustrates the ease of forced admission to the state hospital in the 1950s, using the police as a tool to enforce an unwarranted charge of mental illness.

DAIRY FARMER

An example about which I have personal knowledge is the case of an elderly dairy farmer who had no family and lived alone in a very rural part of the county. He was an infrequent customer of my father's bar, the Jungle Club. Barney maintained a small, profitable dairy farm and lived a solitary life. He was known to go on alcoholic binges a couple of times a year. During one of these binges, he ran afoul of the law and was temporarily committed to Binghamton State Hospital.

When he sobered up and had the hearing without legal or family support, he discovered that he was confined to the hospital for the mandatory sixty days. Poorly educated and with no family to take an interest in him or his case, his farm went untended. The state moved in and sold off his livestock because no one was caring for them. At the end of the sixty-day period, he lost his effort at freedom and was confined indefinitely to the North building, where psychiatric care and evaluation was minimal. Eventually, his farm was sold in a tax sale, and the monies from the farm sale were completely absorbed by the state to pay for his care. He found himself a pauper, confined to a state hospital with little chance of discharge and nowhere to go even if he was discharged. From the North building, he was required to work on the hospital's farm in the Kirkwood area, only a few miles from his lost farm. He passed away in the North building, a broken, bitter man.

I've always wondered how many people in that population of three thousand found themselves in similar straits. This possibility was discussed in heated detail both in class and out, especially by the men in the class, who finally agreed that confinement could happen to any of us. This underlined the adage, "There, but for the grace of God go I." Fortunately, the laws have changed to honor a person's civil rights, though in many cases people are discharged before adequate treatment and become part of the homeless masses.

MEDICAL AND NURSING STAFF

MEDICAL STAFF

Nearly all the physicians were foreign-born Europeans carrying very early twentieth- century medical attitudes. They regarded themselves as the nearest thing to the Second Coming of Christ. Few of them were board certified in psychiatry. The majority was employed in a general residency status, and they were waiting for approval of their applications to practice medicine and enter private practice.

Worse yet were the physician attitudes. More than a few of them required the staff to assemble at the ward entrance to greet them on arrival, treating the staff with disdain. Nearly all spoke broken English and maintained the medical attitude of intellectual and emotional distance from the patient and staff. While making his required rounds of the ward and dayroom, the psychiatrist would be accompanied by the charge nurse, assistant charge nurse, and one or two attendants. Seldom did doctors speak with a patient or respond to a patient's attempt to enter into conversation. Shielding them from the patient was the attendant's duty. If the ward contained bed patients, the doctor would make bedside visits, receiving status reports from the nurse. It was notable that the doctor usually made every effort to avoid physical contact with the patients while examining them. Nearly all drug orders and status comments were dictated to the charge nurse to be transcribed to the chart for the physician's later signature.

The doctors were almost never disturbed during evening or night shifts. Whatever the problem, waiting until morning was the rule of the day. Even deceased patients needed to wait until morning to be officially pronounced dead!

Few physicians obtained any kind of popularity and most were privately mocked, though one stands apart. His name was Kramer. A likeable and personable German, he was unusual in that he had a sense of humor, enjoyed a friendly interaction with the staff, and seemed to really care about the patients. He had been a tank commander early in World War II, and somehow he made the transition to medical school entry. He was not apologetic about his role in the war and actually avoided discussion about it. Doctor Kramer and other doctors lectured the students, but his lectures were the only ones that I enjoyed. His subject was neuroanatomy, and he made it understandable and enjoyable. Maybe that's why I received an A in the class. I should note that his English language skills were good, though with a heavy German accent similar to the B movies of the forties.

One psychiatrist was assigned to each building. He would have a huge office on the ground floor, which he seldom left except to make required ward rounds once a day. Interviews with patients took place in the office and were perfunctory but meeting the legal minimums. The nurse's observations and notes were the only definitive indication of the patient's status and progress, and so the psychiatrist relied heavily on them. This underscores the importance and elevated status of the registered nurse at Binghamton State Hospital.

Beginning with the mansion, built by the famous architect Isaac Perry, the more important members of the medical staff were housed in the beautiful, large homes near the main building on the north side. Additional homes were built opposite Broadmoor and at the entrance to the hospital on Robinson Street. These homes were provided to the doctors as part of their salaries. Of course, patient trustees were assigned the housekeeping assignments.

NURSING STAFF

The female nursing student's cap was exactly like the graduate nurse's cap, minus any stripe along the top. As she progressed through the nursing ranks, the nurse added black stripes denoting rank. For instance, a quarter inch stripe indicated a staff nurse while two stripes indicated a head nurse. A half-inch stripe indicated a feared supervisor of a whole building. Only one nurse wore a one-inch stripe on her cap: the chief supervisor of nurses. Male nurses wore similar, less conspicuous stripes on their right jacket sleeve, similar to navy hash marks. The inch-wide hash mark on the sleeve of the male chief supervisor was equally attention-getting.

Because the physicians freely relinquished their responsibilities to the RNs, the RNs received respect beyond the usual deference. When I entered a ward, I was immediately recognized as a nurse, an authority figure by staff and patients, even though I was a student. It was an exhilarating feeling.

The charge nurse was in charge of the patients and attendants on the ward and answered to the nursing supervisor in charge of the whole building, who responded to the building's physician only for general patient care. The supervisor answered primarily to the chief supervisor, who was in charge of the whole hospital under the hospital administrator. These layers of nursing responsibility were repeated for each of the other two shifts. The daytime charge nurse had overall responsibility.

ATTENDANTS

The nurses at Binghamton State Hospital were similar to the officer corps in the military, and the attendants were the equivalent to the sergeants. Like army sergeants, the attendants were the backbone of patient care and hospital operation. Their responsibilities ranged from bedside nursing to subduing an aggressive patient and taking charge of an entire ward. While the nurses gave overall direction toward operation, the attendants were in daily contact with the patients and set the stage for patient recovery. Acknowledging that there was no specific treatment for mental illness, the attendants augmented the primary treatment, a 'tincture of time', through their kindness and consideration and just lending an ear to the patient's problems. The wards had no separate housekeeping staff so that duty fell to the attendants. Unfortunately, housekeeping was a primary duty while patient care ranked second because the staff was very aware that the condition of the ward was the supervisor's first impression during morning rounds. The criticism of a dirty ward and, of course, dirty patients, would ricochet from the head nurse to the lowest ranking attendant with no excuses accepted.

BINGHAMTON STATE HOSPITAL NURSING PROGRAM

The nursing program at the state hospital was similar to the established registered nursing programs in the country. It provided a three-year nursing program, qualifying graduates for state board exams and becoming a registered nurse. Because Binghamton State Hospital was a psychiatric hospital, it could not provide the legally required minimum medical and surgical clinical experience. Binghamton State Hospital solved that problem by contracting with Bellevue Hospital in New York City, where the second-year students could affiliate there for the whole year. The contract details were unknown, but Bellevue provided the classroom teaching, the clinical experience, and room and board. For two months of the third and final year, another affiliation entailed spending time at Kingston Avenue Hospital in Brooklyn to obtain training and experience in communicable disease nursing.

The three-year program was not similar to college enrollment! Collegiate programs included time away from classes between semesters and a two-month summer vacation. The nursing program, though, was a three-year, full-time program, with two weeks of vacation between each step up to the next level of training. The state required exact levels of classroom lecture and a minimum number of hours of hands-on clinical experience. This mandated a twelve-month, three-year program that barely satisfied the requirements.

State hospitals played host to area nursing programs, helping them to meet state psychiatric nursing requirements. Arnot-Ogden Hospital in Elmira, Binghamton City Hospital, Saint Mary's Hospital in Rochester, and Wilson Memorial Hospital in Johnson City sent their students for their two-month affiliations.

FIRST AUTOPSY

Early in our first year of training, as part of our anatomy and physiology class, we had to attend an autopsy. It was a progression from the frog and cat dissection, where we dealt with hard , board-like, specimens reeking with formaldehyde. Not many autopsies were scheduled because there just was not much interest in autopsies at Binghamton State Hospital. We were fortunate in that one was scheduled on the morning of our anatomy lab class. By chance, our science lab classes were held on the first floor of the laboratory building, and the autopsy operating room was on the same level adjoining the classroom.

With the admonishment to be quiet and to quietly leave if we became sick, we reluctantly strode the fifty feet to the operatory, becoming engulfed in the increasing odor of formaldehyde. I was greeted by the sight of a nude, terribly emaciated, and ghostly white aged female body lying on the hard, white porcelain table with her head resting on a notched board. The pale body barely contrasted with the color of the porcelain operating table. After my initial shock about seeing this elderly, naked woman in the very cold room, I instinctively wanted to cover her with a blanket. Realizing the reality of the situation, I inwardly blushed, and yet, I was proud of my protective instincts.

The operating table had troughs along the perimeter to drain body fluids and water into pails beneath the table. I recall a kitchen-style spring scale and an array of instruments, mostly knives and scissors, located at the head of the table. A formidable-looking circular saw was the only electrical instrument. Facing us, against the wall, was a large sink and counter that held jars filled halfway with clear fluid and with large openings.

The operators consisted of the pathologist and his lab technician assistant. They were waiting for us to assemble before making the first incision. At the sight of the first incision, at least three girls immediately departed the room.

The pathologist gave us an overview of the patient's history and the cause of her death before beginning the autopsy. By the time the torso incisions were completed, widely exposing the abdominal viscera, heart, and lungs, more classmates had departed. While the pathologist was exposing the torso, the lab tech was exposing the skull by peeling the scalp forward from behind and folding it in front of the face. This was planned to make funeral preparations easier by not damaging the face with the scalp dissection. The lab tech then made a cut around the skull and above the ears with a specialized, three-inch oscillating circular electric saw. The saw was special because it only made a cut when the blade encountered bony resistance, thus sparing damage to the brain. When finished, the skull was removed, much as a stocking cap might be removed.

FIRST AUTOPSY

The brain was finally removed by severing the brain stem and placing it on a scale. By this time, there were only a few classmates remaining. I was one of them.

While the pathologist was entering the chest and abdomen, he was lecturing us about the disease process that took the woman's life while also displaying the anatomy and obtaining sections of tissue for the fluid-filled jars.

The woman's fatal disease was colon cancer that had metastasized to her liver and beyond. Her pelvis was a nearly unrecognizable mass, making it impossible to separate organs and demonstrate the anatomy.

By this time, the stench emitting from the body was beginning to overpower me. I managed to handle the horrible sight of the poor woman's body, but the odor of the decaying woman and her body fluids, in addition to the formaldehyde, was about to be too much for me. The pathologist lifted the liver to demonstrate the metastatic lesions. These lesions were sharply defined, elevated, and pale white against the deep red of the liver. From a distance, the lesions looked like mutated flowers that had been placed on the liver. I could persevere no longer. The odor and the sight of the cancer implants on the liver made me lightheaded. I departed as fast as possible, fearing I might faint.

When we finally all reassembled in the classroom, it was time for lunch. Those of us who still felt that we could eat departed for the North building. Food was always served family-style in the dining rooms and in generous portions. This day, the entrée was liver and onions with the lightly colored onions on the deep red liver. It made us recall the dead woman's cancerous liver. That coincidence was the final straw for all of us. Our appetite was destroyed, and we departed. It was as if fate were playing tricks on us. To this day, I cannot eat liver and onions.

FAIRMONT

I was truly grateful to be reassigned from Wagner Hall to Fairmont, the admissions building. Wagner Hall was like hell on earth for the patient still aware of his surroundings, a waiting station before passing through the gates of death. Wagner Hall was, for me, a coarse introduction to the worst element of the human condition, a place where I learned basic nursing procedures under difficult conditions. Once that I was away from Wagner Hall, I was able to attend classes without having to change soiled uniforms.

Fairmont was the gateway to the rest of the hospital or a pause in one's life for two weeks to sixty days or more. Fairmont was primarily a staging area for newly admitted patients, a place where a preliminary diagnostic label was placed after a few interviews.

Fairmont

I was assigned to Ward 63, the male admissions section, as a freshman and later as a senior. When I worked Ward 63 as a freshman and a newbie to the medical field, and especially in psychiatry, I was alternatively overwhelmed and intrigued by the patients and their treatments. It was expected, even demanded, that the students make contact with the patients by simply engaging in conversation with them and attempting to establish a rapport, gleaning background information and charting it. Knowing nothing about psychiatry, I carried the usual unreasonable fears of mental patients that the popular media had generated. That was dispelled after the first few days.

Some cases were heartbreaking because of the terrible disruption mental illness can create in family life. What happened to prompt this patient's admission? What was going on inside the family circle? Would he be fully accepted back into the family at discharge? Would he lose his job? The effect of the patient's admission could be a metaphor for a pebble tossed into a still pond, the spreading waves altering the lives of all in contact with him.

Admission required certification by two doctors, not necessarily psychiatrists, before a person was admitted to the hospital for fifteen days. This allowed a psychiatrist an opportunity to evaluate the patient before a legal hearing for the patient. Following the hearing, the patient could be involuntarily committed for a sixty-day period.

If committed for the sixty-day period, the patient would receive additional psychological testing and in-depth interviews. If the psychiatrist felt that the patient could obtain immediate benefit from definitive treatment, electric shock therapy (electroconvulsive therapy, ECT, or EST) might be attempted. There was little else available to significantly alter the course of a mental illness in the 1950s.

If a course of ECT was felt to benefit the patient, he'd be transferred to a downstairs ward. Following a course of eight to ten ECT treatments, without significant improvement, he would be transferred to one of the interior buildings appropriate to his recovery status. In the interior wards, the patient might receive additional ECTs or other treatment efforts. Failure to recover during the sixty-day period meant that he would be indefinitely committed and transferred deeper into the hospital. The hope was that he would be healed by the passage of time, the so-called tincture of time. He would be offered very little treatment to rescue him from the disease. Beyond the occasional, legally required monthly interviews with the psychiatrist, the patient became a nearly nameless body in the ward, a person filling a bed and a ward roster.

I was impressed with the large number of patients with an overwhelming preoccupation with religion as they descended into deeper mental illness. I wondered at that time if religion was a factor in the development of mental illness or a mental handle to attempt to keep from descending deeper into the chaos of the illness. This conundrum persists for me even today.

One morning, when I reported to the ward, I found out that twins had been admitted. The twins were elderly men, farmers from the nearby Elmira area who had developed a type of schizophrenia that causes a withdrawal from reality and hallucinations in addition to what medicine referred to at that time as senile dementia.

They were so psychically close that they apparently exhibited the same hallucinations and tried to always be together in the ward. They would become agitated if separated. Both of them even awoke at the same time for nature's call, and it was not uncommon to find them sharing the same narrow single bed during night rounds.

Their admission caused a stir in the New York State hospital hierarchy, reaching a psychiatrist who was conducting an ongoing study of mental illness in twins. Within a few days, the twins were transferred. I was never able to follow up on their fate. I wondered how this was accomplished so rapidly. Did the family give transfer permission? Was there any family to consult? Was anyone at all consulted before transfer? As a freshman student, my questions were brushed off, and I was shooed back to my assigned duties.

Alcoholics admitted to the hospital were usually a miserable group. For one thing, they would sober up and become aware in a few hours that they were in a locked ward on State Hospital Hill. For another, after sobering up, they frequently wanted a drink even before clearly establishing their whereabouts. Of course, a drink was not available. In a short while, many would plead for a drink, sometimes becoming aggressive in their efforts to get out of the ward. This might require restraints, making their plights even worse. The only medications available in the 1950s to minimize the withdrawal experience were paraldehyde, chloral hydrate, and barbiturates to control the delirium tremens (DTs) and possible convulsions.

Paraldehyde was given freely every few hours. It seemed to satisfy the alcoholic's desire for a drink since it was metabolized into an aldehyde similar to alcohol, providing sedation.

Entering the ward, it was easy to guess that an alcoholic had been admitted. The pungent odor of paraldehyde permeated the whole ward. That disagreeable odor remained with the patient for days after the last dose. If paraldehyde was even spilled on skin, it would remain there throughout the day like cheap cologne.

Once the alcoholics passed through the drying-out period, they usually remained on Ward 63 until discharged. These patients were then usually model patients. They were helpful around the ward, assisted with other patients, and were above average in intelligence. They would be interviewed three or four times by the resident psychiatrist to establish a diagnosis and discover any serious underlying emotional disorder. That would be the extent of treatment.

Patient or family counseling or group counseling to help the patient remain sober was practically unheard of. And if it was heard of, it was given lip service only as the staff was too weighed down with sheer numbers of patients to provide such care. The treatment goal seemed to be centered only on drying out the patient and discharging him back to the community. Usually the patient was only given booklets about Alcoholics Anonymous and advised to attend meetings.

Yet there were alcoholics who developed a chronic dementia due to long-time alcoholism or who had an underlying mental illness. They would be retained in the hospital for an indefinite period, frequently for the rest of their lives. These patients were incapable of independent living and adapted well to the institutionalized, structured life the hospital provided.

BROADMOOR

My next assignment was Broadmoor. I thought I was accustomed to the state hospital atmosphere, but Broadmoor brought forth anxiety based on its rumored history. It was four stories tall and full of men in a kind of psychiatric hell. The old, foreboding red brick building had heavy wire netting across all the windows and floor-to-ceiling wire netting on the porches. As one approached the building in warm weather, the open windows and porches allowed shouts, screams, and pleadings to emerge. These sounds mingled unintelligibly, making the approach a chilling experience. No effort was ever made to landscape around the building, which only added to the gloomy façade. The peeling paint on the windows enhanced the effect. Once inside, with the doors shut and each ward locked, it became surreally quiet. It seemed that everywhere one looked, there was heavy steel mesh fence. With no elevators, the stairwells resembled a windowless caged cave. The painted woodwork was faded and peeling, and the once beautifully stained walnut wood entrance and stairwell had aged to a dark brown with gouges and scratches.

Broadmoor

Patients were assigned to a ward in Broadmoor after the failed cursory psychiatric treatment in Fairmont or after becoming unmanageable in another building. They were issued the hospital-made denim jumpsuit, cloth slippers, and no underwear. If the patient was alert, cooperative, and able to care for himself, he could wear street clothing that his family might have brought to him and would be assigned to a more civilized ward. Installed in a Broadmoor ward, he was ready to essentially heal himself with the passage of time or proceed to deteriorate into a vegetative state.

My first assignment in Broadmoor was Ward 46. It was the medical ward and was divided into three parts: a huge dayroom, a dormitory, and a nursing unit with bed patients. Usually, there were only about ten to fifteen bed patients. The rest, numbering about forty patients, were up and about with various forms of mental deterioration and physical ailments.

The permanent staff consisted of a head nurse and four attendants. The attendants were always glad to see the student nurses arrive since they could turn over the care of the bed patients to the students and could spend time in the ward's shower/bathroom, the smoking area. They apparently felt that their job was to maintain order and follow the ward routine of cleaning, feeding, and keeping the peace.

I hasten to note that most of the wards were supervised solely by attendants. These wards, managed by attendants only, were models of cleanliness and efficiency. That was the goal of the attendants, ever-aware that the nurse supervising the building might arrive at any moment for critical appraisal. It was not their goal to interact with the patients except to encourage them to conform to ward routine. After a variable period, a new admission would be appropriately dulled to the ward routine and would fall in lockstep with the rest of the patients. Few of the attendants made any serious effort to connect with the patients. They had their routines and eight hours to put in before going home.

But the attendants did invariably treat the patients with respect and kindness. The student nurses, on the other hand, were expected to attempt to make intellectual contact or simply to try to communicate with the patients on any level. I relished, with some reservations, the interaction with the patients.

I witnessed my first grand mal seizure there. It was my questionably good fortune to be standing next to the patient in the dayroom when he moaned and fell to the floor, all his muscles rigid. When he landed, his head must have arrived first because blood started gushing from the back of his head. With my shout for help, everyone came running, including the aware patients. He had turned lightly cyanotic and finally started breathing as he entered the clonic (jerking) phase of the convulsion, which continued for what seemed an eternity. I was sent to the nurse's station to mix 500 milligrams of sodium amytal, a barbiturate, in a 20-cc syringe. The charge RN gave a portion of it intravenously, which stopped the convulsion. I found out that it was unusual to intervene with drugs, instead, they would just allow the convulsion to follow its course while protecting the patient during the seizure. The sight of a grand mal seizure is a most frightening thing to see. The hypersalivation and sometimes blood from injuries adds to the impressive scene. Happily, this patient recovered well, and his laceration was minor.

A patient in a vegetative state, by the 1950 definition, meant that he would frequently assume an intrauterine position, was uncommunicative, frequently hallucinated, was occasionally combative, and was incontinent for urine and feces. The patient could frequently be seen playing with or eating his feces. These patients, out of necessity, wore the coarse coveralls and no underwear. On very warm days, the attendants would allow those patients to be nude, covering their genitals with a bath towel. Caring for these patients included frequent showering with changes of coveralls and spoon-feeding each meal. A third of Ward 46 patients were probably in this condition. Showering these soiled patients involved transferring them to an extremely heavy oak rocking chair, placing specially made wheels under the rockers, tipping the rocking chair onto the wheels, and rolling him into the shower. There he would be washed with a showerhead on a hose and dressed in fresh coveralls.

Wearing a white uniform with white buck shoes was out of place in caring for these patients. Many days I would have to return to Ferris Hall and change uniforms before going to class. It would not be good form to attend class smeared with feces or with a fecal odor about you!

I observed my first catatonic schizophrenia patient on Ward 46. He was standing in the back of the ward, immobile and mute, with his arms in the air. There was saliva dripping from his mouth, his expression was vacant, and his eyes were fixed with only occasional blinking. He would maintain any posture he was placed in except he would change position to maintain his balance. Of course, he was incontinent and had to be spoon-fed. He would not respond to pinching or a needle stick. It was said that while catatonic patients are in this apparent stuporous state, they could recall verbatim emotionally charged comments made in previous days when emerging from the immobility in days and weeks previous. Many such patients would aggressively confront employees and other patients whom they felt were abusive during the catatonia. The catatonic patient frequently emerges into a manic state with aggressive outbursts that may last for a few minutes or days. It was shocking to first observe this particular patient and hard to believe that anyone could remain nearly immobile and completely mute for such long periods.

I was rotated to Broadmoor on a number of occasions. Each time, I entered with an air of foreboding, submerged fear, and smoldering depression. It was not uncommon for a quiet patient to suddenly become aggressive and attempt to strike out or throw some object or body fluid at others in response to his hallucinations or delusions. Psychiatric nursing in this building boiled down to maintaining order, showering soiled patients, and preventing them from hurting themselves or others.

I always disliked that the ward-assigned GE table radio was playing music in the nursing stations instead of in the huge dayrooms. The dayrooms were stark in a predominate color of gray. They usually measured about thirty by fifty feet, with many large windows covered with a heavy steel wire mesh. Many patients had to sit on the floor because there were not enough chairs or heavy oak rocking chairs. No efforts were made to decorate the dayrooms. There were no curtains, shades, or furnishings other than the chairs and a couple of oak study tables. Including such décor was a possible hazard in this setting. Each dayroom in the building had a pendulum clock hanging higher than one could reach. It must have dated to the turn of the century. Without any sound absorption material in the room, each tick of the clock was loud enough to be heard throughout the dayroom. I wondered if the clock was placed in these dayrooms for the calming effect of the ticking in addition to keeping the patients somewhat oriented as to time. No calendar could be seen in any of the dayrooms to help patients retain date orientation so every day seemed the same. There were no pictures on the walls. If a magazine turned up in the dayroom, it was immediately snatched by an aware patient and tucked into his coveralls. In Broadmoor, no effort was made to provide any entertainment or diversion to stimulate a patient's interest outside of the dreary routine. For the patients who were aware of their environments, each day seemed like any other, day after day after day, a stultifying existence that only hastened emotional decay. These formerly aware patients developed a kind of institutional psychosis that was displayed in apathy and lack of emotional response overlaid onto their basic mental illnesses.

Ambulatory patients who were hyperactive were given a floor polisher to push back and forth in the dayroom. The polisher was a ten-pound stiff brush measuring about twelve by eighteen inches and was attached to a six-foot hinged handle. Some of the patients who were deeply involved in their hallucinations would push the polisher back and forth all day, stopping only at the insistence of the attendants for meals and hygiene. This was the only exercise that patients received in those back wards. The polished hardwood floors in the dayrooms of all the ambulatory wards would be the admiration of the most fastidious homemaker. No effort was made to encourage physical activity. Most attendants were satisfied if a patient involved within his hallucinations remained seated all day. The polished hardwood floors in the dayrooms of all the ambulatory wards would be the admiration of the most fastidious homemaker.

On the wholly ambulatory wards, the patients were led down the wire-enclosed stairwells to a dining room and were served cafeteria-style. The dish was a segmented tin plate with a teaspoon as the only utensil, and both were collected and inventoried at meal's end. The food frequently was unrecognizable, and when the patient arrived at the end of the food line, his food overlapped into an unappetizing pile. It was a regular occurrence for a hallucinating patient to aggressively begin throwing his plate at an imagined sight, which might be another patient. That was when a melee might break out. It was not unlike the jail scenes in B movies of the 1930s. Days spent on the ward and descents into the dining room comprised their whole world. Mealtime was a high point in a patient's day. It was an opportunity to have a change of scenery and activity.

Ward 51 on the top floor was the most feared. It held the most aggressive patients of any in Broadmoor or the whole hospital for that matter. Uncontrollably aggressive patients were relegated to Ward 51. Of course the biggest attendants were assigned there to maintain control.

Entrance into the dayroom of Ward 51 was a frightening experience. When a visitor entered the ward, especially a white-uniformed nurse, many of the patients would crowd about the person to just stare, especially if the nurse was female. The arrival was a break in the mind-numbing routine. This required the attendants to rescue the guest by scattering the gathered patients. I was only assigned to Ward 51 for two weeks, but it was an unforgettable experience.

There were always eight or ten patients in camisoles (commonly called straitjackets) mingling with other patients, hallucinating, cursing, and even trying to fight anyone who came near them. The rest of the patients were sitting on hard benches, pacing, or sitting on the floor. Some were withdrawn yet would burst into a frenzy of activity at any moment, while most were agitated and aggressively pursuing their hallucinations. Sedatives, such as barbiturates or chloral hydrate, could only be administered over a short term. There was no other psychically active medication in the early 1950s.

I recall the two most feared patients were long-time residents of Ward 51. One huge Slavic fellow named Ski would rather fight than eat. A person had to always be on guard when nearing him or attempting to talk with him. Without any warning, he would direct a huge fist your way. An interesting thing about Ski was that he never attacked anyone from behind but always face to face. The other most feared patient was a paraplegic black man who dragged himself about the dayroom, inviting one and all to fight. He was the most feared, a schizophrenic completely involved in his hallucinations and with huge upper body development from dragging himself about. If no one accepted an invitation to fight, he would simply attack someone—anyone—scattering everyone nearby.

This was the only ward in which one could see more than just a few patients in camisoles or restraint sheets. Restraint sheets are laced, heavy canvas sheeting that the patient is forced beneath. The canvas is laced to the bed with a hole in the upper canvas for the patient's head. The camisole is a canvas jacket with closed, overly long sleeves. The patient's arms are inserted into the jacket, which is laced in the back, and the arms are crossed across the chest and tightly tied behind the patient.

State law required a patient to be released from both types of restraint at regular intervals and that this be documented. As might be guessed, the regular intervals were frequently stretched for the most aggressive patients, though the patient's chart would reflect that they were released as required.

With the exception of Ward 46 and Ward 51, the rest of Broadmoor's wards were filled with psychiatrically deteriorating schizophrenic patients. One exception was at least one ward full of failed lobotomy patients, which deserves special mention later.

Broadmoor could best be summed up as the nearest thing to the living version of Dante's Inferno. Special mention must be made here, and will be made again later, that in the 1950s, there were no antipsychotic drugs available and no long-term safe sedatives available. With treatment lacking, there was nothing else to do but to allow patients full reign to suffer the agonies of psychosis and for the care to be protecting them from harm.

The public was unaware of the unbelievable conditions at Broadmoor, and those who were aware seldom discussed the conditions. Patients assigned to Broadmoor seldom received monthly visitors, the family members having essentially written them out of their lives after years of failed treatment or the lack of it. This fractured family connection was just another nail in the coffin of isolation and desertion that the patient must have felt. The patients of the 1950s aged and expired there or were transferred to the newer Garvin building. Broadmoor still exists today, empty but easily recognizable from the above description of the exterior.

ELECTRIC SHOCK THERAPY

In 1937, an Italian neurologist named Ugo Cerletti teamed with Lucio Bini and L. B. Kalinowski to develop the technique of electric shock therapy. The Cerletti-Bini approach was introduced to the United States in 1939, achieving spectacular success. Ninety percent of cases of severe depression, which were resistant to all treatments, disappeared after three to four weeks of ECT.

While assigned to Fairmont, I was exposed to a treatment favored by psychiatrists, electric shock therapy (electcroconvulsive therapy, ECT, EST). Most of the shock treatments were given here. Since ECT was one of the few treatments available, it was not uncommon for newly admitted psychotic patients to be given a trial series of ten shocks. Lacking other definitive treatment, a course of ECT was routinely utilized as one of those "maybe it will help" treatments.

Electric shock therapy (EST) or electro-convulsive therapy (ECT) became one of the main forms of treatment for the manic depressive and involutional psychoses before 1960. It was also useful for some forms of schizophrenia, with variable results.

Throughout my training at Binghamton State Hospital, I participated in hundreds of ECT treatments. I likened it in my mind to the Puritan cold water public dunking used for shock treatment of the insane. As a peon in the treatment structure, there was nothing I could do to change the routine, and I wasn't brilliant enough to offer an alternative therapy.

The team consisted of six people, including the doctor. Two people lined up on each side of the table, with the nurse at the head and the doctor to operate the machine. A padded table was set up at the far end of a dormitory hallway, deliberately selected as most distant from the patient entrance, a distance of possibly fifty feet. I was always appalled at the primitive manner in which the patient was made to approach the treatment table. The patient would be led down the hallway with up to three attendants to guide him to the table. The attendants would have very little to say to the patient except to sharply encourage him to continue to the table. The aware patient, if it was his first treatment, would be terribly frightened of the unknown treatment he was about to receive. The sight of the ECT team grimly staring at him at the end of the hall only heightened the fear.

Placing the frightened, resisting patient on the table sometimes took the efforts of the whole team. When finally the patient was lying on the table, each team member would support an extremity, and the doctor or nurse would place a bite block in the mouth. It was made of tongue depressors wrapped with gauze and placed in the mouth width-wise so that the cheeks were distorted. The patient was told to bite on it while the nurse held the jaw tightly closed. It was then that conductive jelly would be liberally applied to the temples, and the doctor would apply the silver dollar-size electrodes, holding them in place with a latex band. Later models of the apparatus would speed the procedure by using a large caliper that looked like ice tongs. A baseball-size wire mesh ball covered with gauze soaked in conductive gel was on each end.

The doctor would squeeze the tong ends against the patient's temples and, when assured that the team was ready, he would throw the switch on the black box, passing electricity through the patient's scalp, bone, and brain to the other electrode on the opposite temple. Immediately, the patient's body entered a grand mal seizure, the tonic phase first, in which every skeletal muscle entered a spasm and stiffened the body. After what seemed an eternity, the patient entered the clonic phase of the seizure, where those same muscles developed a rhythmic jerking movement. Another seeming eternity passed, and the patient entered an unconscious relaxed phase. During the convulsion, the team members on each side of the table were responsible for supporting the extremities but not restraining the limbs to prevent injury. Occasional spinal fractures occurred during the convulsive tonic phase and were discovered long after treatment.

It was common that, on the first treatment, the black box settings would not produce a convulsion, and the patient would not even lose consciousness. It would then be necessary to increase the voltage, amperage, and current duration through experimentation until a grand mal convulsion ensued. Once the convulsive threshold was reached, it was recorded for future treatments. Sometimes multiple attempts were required to establish the threshold, undoubtedly at great psychological pain to the patient.

Upon completion of the seizure, the patient entered a very relaxed, unconscious state. It was very common for the patient to experience a brief respiratory arrest. This slow return of spontaneous respiration sometimes became alarming, since respirations ceased at the beginning of the seizure. As the patient developed a deepening cyanosis, the doctor would authoritatively step up to the patient and lightly thump the area of the epigastrium a few times to initiate breathing. Failing this maneuver, one could sense the rapidly increasing panic developing, and a nervous doctor would then compress the chest with both hands. Fortunately, all the patients resumed spontaneous breathing during the treatments in which I attended. There was never equipment to assist respiration nearby. There was no one present, including the doctor, trained in respiratory management until the late 1950s. Although there was usually an oxygen tank nearby, it was of little use in dealing with apnea without a means of positive pressure ventilation.

When the doctor was satisfied that the patient was stable, a stretcher would be brought alongside the table, and the patient was moved onto it. He would be placed on his side and wheeled into a separate dormitory, where a nurse and an attendant would watch over him until awakening. Monitoring vital signs was considered unnecessary.

Upon awakening, the patient would be amnesiac, confused, and sometimes aggressive. It was not uncommon for the nurse to be nearly overwhelmed in attempting to deal with six or eight patients in varying stages of awakening.

ELECTRIC SHOCK THERAPY

Usually, in less than thirty minutes, the patient could be led into the dayroom, where an attendant would casually observe him, as would his fellow patients. This amnesia would persist for much of the day, and the patient would be very tractable and passive, gradually resuming his pretreatment demeanor and even showing signs of improvement. It was interesting to note that there was a noticeable change in the other patients in the dayroom, a change in activity and a lower noise level on those ECT days.

The ECT treatments were usually prescribed in a block of ten, with the ECT given twice a week. After the first treatment, the patients gradually remembered the experience and reacted with understanding terror. They would attempt to strongly resist getting the treatment or would be reduced to pleading and tears. I feel sure the patient must have felt like a prisoner walking the last mile to the electric chair.

In later years, experimentation with direct current equipment and varying voltage/amperage/duration settings resulted in no significant change in results from the older alternating current machines.

Why was no sedative given to make the treatment less terrifying? There was a theory at that time that the very act of the long, conscious walk to the table for the ECT was as therapeutic as the ECT itself. The walk to the table was likened in psychiatric theory to a subconscious punishment for imagined misdeeds or a stress-shock to the unconscious mind, helping to snap the patient out of his psychosis. Another reason for the avoidance of a barbiturate sedative was the fear that the barbiturate would raise the convulsive threshold, which was considered necessary for successful treatment.

In 1953, when I returned from my Bellevue training, impressions had changed and the patients were given the benefit of sedative, a low dose of chloral hydrate. This made a difference in patient acceptance of the treatment. In later years, a nurse anesthetist (CRNA) would administer anesthesia just prior to the ECT. The chosen anesthetic would be intravenous Pentothal or Brevital, which produced unconsciousness, and succinylcholine to completely relax the muscles, including muscles of respiration. He would then manually hyperventilate the patient with oxygen, stepping aside for the ECT. With the completion of the treatment, the anesthetist would immediately resume controlled respiration until the drugs were metabolized and respiration resumed. Another big advance, previously considered unnecessary, was that the nurse anesthetist (CRNA) maintained open intravenous access throughout the entire procedure, enabling administration of additional medications to cope with any emergency. The patient still experienced the grand mal seizure, though the outward appearances of the tonic and clonic phases would not be seen. Gone were the infrequent fractures caused by the muscle spasms. The patients awakened in much the same manner, with confusion and short-term amnesia. The older psychiatrists said that treatment success with sedation was less effective than the "cold turkey" approach. Possibly so, but I felt that using the sedative/anesthetic approach was a more merciful and safer treatment path. A disadvantage to this sympathetic approach was that while the anesthetic produced total muscle relaxation, it was never positively known whether the convulsive threshold was reached. That threshold was considered essential for successful therapy.

I've often wondered just what effect the electric current had on the brain to cause this alteration in emotional function. It seems that using 120 AC volts at varying amperage, flowing for 0.1 of a second or more to produce a convulsion, must have caused a degree of irreparable changes in the brain that may have become apparent in later years.

After a series of ten or more ECT treatments in which the patient showed little change and after the initial diagnosis and psychotherapy at Fairmont, he would then be transferred to another building suited to the depth of his condition to make room for new admissions. He would be placed in custodial care status, with only sporadic visits with the building's psychiatrist. The subsequent use of ECT on these patients would be limited to controlling disruptive behavior. Thus would begin the possible downward spiral of these patients in their mental illnesses.

My sporadic observations during the 1950s were generally positive toward ECT treatments. I have seen dramatic changes in patients with severe manic depressive and involutional psychoses. These patients seemed to quickly return to normal-appearing activity and emotional responses. This enabled the doctor to counsel the patients still assigned to Fairmont, even allowing many of them to be discharged before completion of the sixty-day commitment. Still, I've agonized over the terror that these patients experienced as they approached the ECT treatment table and the depth of the loss of their memories.

INSULIN SHOCK THERAPY

Insulin shock therapy was another level of treatment for the mentally ill. Patients chosen for this treatment were mostly the nondeteriorated schizophrenics. It was believed that the severe alteration in the body chemistry from high doses of insulin would cause a reversal in the psychosis. I noted a significant number of remissions during my tenure on the floor.

The benefits of insulin shock therapy (ICT/IST) was discovered serendipitously in 1931 when Doctor Sakel, from Vienna, observed a marked improvement in diabetic psychotic patients he was treating for opiate addiction and who were accidentally given overdoses of insulin, causing them to enter into a coma. Insulin shock therapy came to the United States in the late thirties and enjoyed intense use in treatment for schizophrenia until the midseventies.

I was assigned to the insulin shock (IST)/electric shock (ECT) unit at the main building as a graduate nurse while I was awaiting state board test results. Much of this therapy in the hospital was now centered here and made this ward a very busy place.

A typical treatment unit would consist of six to eight patients who ranged from initial entrant to those deep into the insulin treatment program. By having patients who were at different levels in the regimen, the intense recovery phase during a treatment would be graduated, safer, and less intense for the team. Twenty IST treatments per patient were the usual number, and after a period of rest, the patient would be transferred to another ward for evaluation.

A typical day in the IST unit would consist of each patient being given his prescribed intramuscular dose of regular insulin. A new patient would usually receive five to ten units, which increased each day by significant doses based on the previous day's effects. When the dosage that produced unconsciousness was reached, it usually remained at that level throughout the treatment.

A patient would arrive early in the unit, without breakfast and dressed in a hospital gown. He was assigned a bed. Patients who were well into treatment received insulin without fear and were usually very manageable. This contrasted sharply with electric shock therapy, which was intense and dramatic and had a hazy recovery. Within an hour, the patient receiving the higher insulin dose would drift into unconsciousness and remain in that state ideally for another hour. Patients receiving lower doses would develop lesser symptoms such as confusion, sweating, and mild tremors. Predicting the depth of the coma from each daily dose could not be reasonably determined, since the patient's liver glycogen stores could not be calculated. After two hours, we would give 50 percent glucose to the conscious patients to drink. The unconscious patients received intravenous 10 percent glucose at a low rate until arousal. The treatment would be immediately aborted in patients who entered a convulsive state. Placing a steel needle in a vein in the arm would sometimes be extremely difficult due to the convulsive movements. Maintaining the IV access was also difficult because only steel needles were in use in those years and were easily dislodged by the tremors.

Terminating the therapy when convulsions occurred was an intense period, sometimes requiring efforts of the whole team to restrain the patient, maintain an airway, and struggle to obtain venous access. The veins became less available during succeeding convulsive episodes because of bruising and damage to the blood vessels.

The use of rubber nasogastric (stomach) tubes to terminate the coma, though in use at some centers, was not a consideration. There was the problem of patient cooperation to insert the tube at each therapy session and the hazard of accidental dislodgement and reinsertion into the lung. Inadvertent placement of 50 percent glucose solution into the lung would produce a severe pulmonary complication. In addition, glucose solution correctly placed into the stomach carried the hazard of aspiration through regurgitation during an unconscious/convulsive period.

Continuous IV maintenance during the treatment period was not feasible because an infusion in a glass container had to be maintained at a minimal flow rate to avoid clotting of the needle in the patient's immobilized arm. In addition, these psychotic patients frequently would not tolerate an infusion and an indwelling IV needle. The use of capped, flexible IV catheters was not introduced until a decade later. This placement of an IV catheter prior to a daily dose would have easily allowed the session to be aborted.

There was also an economic bottom line preventing continuous IV infusions: cost. While the downtown hospitals had disposable plastic infusion sets, the state would not provide enough funding for all infusions to utilize the plastic IV sets. The infusion equipment had to be prepared by Central Supply, using glass drip chambers, latex hoses, and glass needle connectors attached with silk ties.

After assurances that the patient was conscious and stable, we would direct them to the shower, feed them a high-carbohydrate meal, and closely observe them for the next few hours. It was not uncommon for a patient to re-enter a coma from not having been given enough oral carbohydrate to cover the insulin administered.

As with ECT, insulin shock therapy was gradually sidetracked in favor of pharmacological treatment introduced in 1954.

LOBOTOMY

Lobotomy, or leucotomy, is the surgical undercutting of the frontal lobe of the brain. It was developed by Egas Moniz in 1935 to relieve severe agitation and obsessive–compulsive behavior. It was soon directed to patients with schizophrenia. During the 1940s and 1950s, prefrontal lobotomy, a surgical approach via the patient's temporal region, was widely used. During those years, hundreds of lobotomies were performed at Binghamton State Hospital and other mental hospitals in the country.

My contact with the procedure occurred during my first year rotation through surgery at Binghamton State Hospital. The preparation for the procedure was a startling sight. The patient, awake, unsedated, and restrained, with head shaven, was placed on the operating table. An IV was started and intravenous sedatives might be used to quiet patient movements. The surgeon used local anesthesia to prepare the scalp for the apparatus that was to be attached to the patient's head by screws applied directly into the cranium. The attached instrument contained a ring that circled the patient's head and had adjustable brackets extending from the ring on both sides of the head. The adjustable brackets precisely guided the direction that the knife must travel into the brain. When the hardware was in place, the surgeon made two incisions into the temporal scalp and used a trephine (circular saw) to drill a very small hole into the cranium. The surgeon, guided by the preoperative calculation, then passed the special knife into the frontal lobe of the brain, severing the connection of the frontal lobe to the rest of the brain with coarse movements of the knife. While the procedure gave the impression of scientific precision, it was at best a crude surgical maneuver to sever unknown pathways in the brain.

The patient was observed on the surgical ward for a couple of days and then returned to the assigned ward. Unfortunately, lobotomy was no cure of psychoses. These patients retained the basic psychosis, including the delusions and hallucinations. Lobotomy did make the patient tractable and communication possible, whereas before the lobotomy, the patient might have been unapproachable.

The postlobotomy patient would fail to physically respond to psychotic impulses or would do so seemingly in slow motion. For instance, the act of striking out at someone would be very slow in developing. As for daily activities, the patient would be very malleable and conform to the ward routine without objections. Such was the criterion for a successful lobotomy.

I recall a patient nicknamed Ski, who was a resident of Ward 51 for years. He was so aggressive and assaultive that he was always approached with extreme care because he would strike without warning. He experienced a total change following lobotomy, becoming very passive and docile with almost no intellectual curiosity. It became easy to manage Ski, but the lobotomy did nothing to cure his schizophrenia. Ski was discharged from Ward 51 and reassigned to a long-term custodial ward.

Two wards—one for males and one for females—were populated by the lobotomy failures. These wards were the worst in the hospital. The patients would be in varying levels of vegetative existence. They could be found dressed in the hospital-made coveralls and sitting on the floor in an intrauterine position with knees drawn up to their chins and arms wrapped about them. The patients might be incontinent and play with feces, completely unaware of the world around them. They were the occupants of the "back ward" in the most negative sense, the forgotten humans.

In the mid-1950s, transorbital lobotomy replaced the prefrontal lobotomy as the technique of choice. Theoretically, the transorbital approach was more selective in severing the frontal lobe and caused less disastrous results.

When I was assigned to the electric/insulin shock unit as a new graduate, it frequently was my responsibility to operate the electric shock "black box." That is, I operated the equipment as ordered by the doctor, attached the electrodes to the patient, and initiated the convulsive treatment.

When a transorbital lobotomy was scheduled, I would transport the black box to the operating room, where the patient and doctor would be waiting with the OR nurse. It was not necessary to shave the patient's head. After the patient was positioned and secured on the OR table, I attached the electrodes to the temples, placed the bite block in his mouth, and administered the convulsive shock. When the patient's convulsion ended and somnolence followed, the nurse quickly prepped the eyes with PHisoHex soap. The doctor was handed an instrument calibrated in centimeters that had the appearance of an ice pick. It was inserted under each upper lid, and, using a hammer, the doctor drove it through the bone behind the eye and into the frontal lobe. There was no mechanical guide to indicate the angle of entry, just the depth. The instrument would be moved back and forth an arbitrary distance as the doctor felt necessary. If the patient were to emerge from the electric shock and begin movement, I would administer another convulsive dose. This was my first anesthetic experience and increased my desire to enter anesthesia training. Of course, these patients recovering on the surgical ward could be easily recognized because they had huge black eyes.

Despite the most unscientific technique for transorbital lobotomy, the success rate was amazingly high and much better than the temporal route. There were fewer total failures resulting in the patient being warehoused in the back ward at Broadmoor. On the contrary, many of these patients seemed to be relieved of their psychotic symptoms and were, in many cases, alert, cooperative, and sociable. It should also be noted that some of these patients were able to return to their previous lifestyles, though most were either retained within the hospital's care or relocated to a custodial facility.

Lobotomy later fell into disrepute because of the lack of consistent positive results and the large number of catastrophic complications. It was replaced with the advent of new mind-altering drugs in the late 1950s that, in many cases, resulted in a sort of reversible pharmacological lobotomy from the huge doses usually administered.

HYDROTHERAPY

Hydrotherapy, or treatment with water, was not actually a treatment for mental illness but a way to calm the agitated or aggressive patient.

WET SHEET

The leading hydrotherapy for these patients was the wet sheet. It was nearly the last resort when all else failed to control the aggressive impulses. The patient was forced to lie on a stretcher upon which ten or fifteen wet, cold sheets that had been soaking in ice water were previously arranged. As one can imagine, placing a fighting patient on the wet, cold stretcher and enveloping him with the sheets required the efforts of a number of burly attendants. Each sheet was individually and tightly wrapped about the patient from shoulder to toe until all sheets were interwoven about him, leaving only the head and feet visible. The patient looked like a living mummy. Finally, a leather restraint sheet was placed over the patient and laced to the bed.

Initially the patient might be cursing and fighting the procedure, but that gradually tapered to a few mutterings and chattering of teeth from the cold sheets. Amazingly, the active resistance of the patient and the insulation of the cold sheets increased the patient's core temperature to sometimes frightening levels. Patient safety demanded constant monitoring, especially of body temperature. Accurate body temperature measurement was difficult since there was no axillary or rectal access, and oral temperatures were not safe because only glass thermometers were available. After a few hours in the wet sheet, the exhausted and enervated patient emerged very manageable. It was not a surprise that even the most aggressive patients, who were nearly out of touch with reality, could frequently be calmed with just the threat of the wet sheet after having had a few exposures to the sheeting. Those same patients also knew that only the male nurse in charge had the authority to offer the threat with any meaning.

CONTINUOUS TUB BATH

The reasonably cooperative, nonaggressive patient would be placed in a large bathtub filled with water slightly above the patient's body temperature. The tub would contain a canvas sling to hold the patient suspended in the tub. Frequently, restraints would be necessary to prevent the patient from moving out of the tub. Prior to immersion, the nude patient would be coated with mineral oil to minimize skin maceration. Once in the tub and submerged in water, a leather sheet would be placed over the patient's body and attached to the tub, with only a hole for his head. The patient would remain in the water bath for a few hours, and this succeeded in calming most patients. The continuous tub bath was not a favored treatment method since the equipment occupied a large space and intense monitoring was required for safety.

SALT GLOW AND SCOTCH DOUCHE

Very wet salt would be vigorously rubbed over every inch of the body. When completed, the patient would stand in a shower stall that had at least six needle-spray showerheads. The water emerged at body temperature and at a slightly uncomfortable high pressure.

From a distance of about fifteen feet, an operator would concurrently spray the patient's back with water (Scotch douche) from a high-pressure hose. The shower and spray times would vary depending on the patient's response. When the patient emerged, he would feel calmed and depleted. His skin would feel extremely smooth from the vigorous scrubbing with the salt. An hour or so later, the depleted feeling would give way to a feeling of well-being.

The Scotch douche has been popular in European spas and was mildly useful psychiatric care because of the circulatory stimulation and psychic calming of the high-pressure spray.

PSYCHOPHARMACY

In the mid-1950s, the prevailing treatments, such as insulin and electric shock therapy, hydrotherapy, and lobotomy, were essentially displaced by the introduction of psychoactive medications. These medications, reserpine and chlorpromazine, revolutionized the treatment of the mentally ill. These drugs made the patients approachable for psychotherapy by calming them and disconnecting them somewhat from their diseases.

The number of wards containing aggressive, hyperactive, and uncontrollable patients were greatly diminished. The ward population was replaced by those who exhibited little innovation in activity and an emotional response that resembled a chemically induced lobotomy. A large number of them required huge doses of chlorpromazine to alter their behaviors and frequently resulted in multiple, severe complications, such as liver damage and occasionally irreversible neuromuscular changes. A ward that previously held hypcractivc, hallucinating, and poorly controlled patients now contained residents quietly responding to their hallucinations. Some had deep jaundice and showed tremors similar to Parkinson's disease.

Patients unresponsive to the minimal psychotherapy provided were, nonetheless, relatively easy to control and amenable to the ward routine. The success of these two drugs initiated a windfall of new psychiatrically active drugs that completely changed the environment and treatment of the mentally ill. The use of these drugs allowed many to return to society and lead productive lives.

The success of the psychoactive drugs dramatically lowered the patient census at Binghamton State Hospital from three thousand plus to a few hundred. The hospital was then able to transfer patients to the nearly new Garvin building and essentially close down the remainder of the hospital campus. Over time, even the Garvin building lost occupants to the success of the new drugs, and the building was nearly empty. Later, the state leased part of the Garvin building to the Veterans Administration for general outpatient care and to SUNY (State University of New York) for medical training, still leaving a substantial portion unoccupied.

SURGERY AND CENTRAL SUPPLY

Surgery was located between Ward 6 and Ward 5 (a female ward) with a connecting hall and another hallway to the main building. To enter the ramp to the main building or to Ward 5 or Ward 6, one had to pass through the surgical department, instrument storage, and the minor OR on one side and the major OR and Central Supply on the other side. To enter the major OR, one had to enter through the Central Supply and sterilization prep area, which contained the autoclaves, wrapping table, and surgical scrub sinks.

Upon entering the OR, the odor of wet, scorched cloth struck the nose forcefully. It was generated by the autoclave steam on the cloth-wrapped equipment packs. When surgery was in progress, the very pungent odor of the anesthetic, ether, also blended into the mix.

The major operating room had a twelve to fourteen foot ceiling with a skylight directly over the OR table.

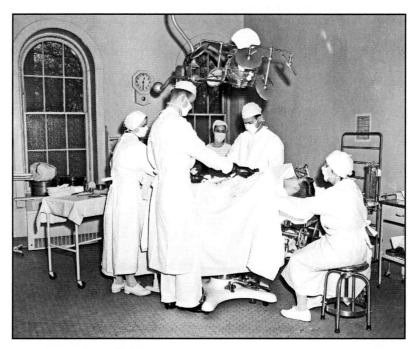

Operating Room

At the far end of the room was a double-hung window. The room lacked air conditioning, so on a hot summer day this window would be opened and a fan placed in front of it to draw in cool air. It seemed that personal and patient comfort trumped possible contamination of the surgical field with unfiltered, outside air circulating through the OR!

The surgical light was suspended from the ceiling on an angled bar over the operating table. It was a twenty four inch sphere with lenses positioned about its surface. The lenses focused on four or five fixed mirrors that were attached to the sphere approximately two feet from it. The mirrors reflected light to a central point. This reflected light was in addition to the sphere's main light focus.

SURGERY AND CENTRAL SUPPLY

The function of this surgical light was to provide light from many angles, eliminating shadows in the surgical field. With a single supporting beam from the ceiling, the light could be positioned in an almost complete circle. Each morning, when reporting for duty, it was the responsibility of the student to wipe the surface of the light with a cloth saturated with absolute (98 percent) alcohol.

All the frequently used instruments, including a major and minor laparotomy (lap) instrument pack, were pre-wrapped, autoclaved, and arrayed about the OR, ready for immediate use. If a necessary instrument became contaminated during surgery, it was necessary to sterilize it in boiling water for twenty minutes. This frequently created great angst because the surgeon had to wait for sterilization and thus extended the surgical/anesthesia time with its hazards. The three-minute flash autoclave, which used high-pressure steam sterilization, was yet to be developed. When sterilized, the instrument was carried to the OR table with large forceps, the tips of which were continually soaked in 70 percent alcohol.

The OR table had hydraulic pedals and round cranks extending to the head of the table to allow the anesthetist to adjust the table to the position desired by the surgeon. The table was essentially the same as modern tables that now use electric motors for the same adjustments.

The last major piece of equipment in the OR was the anesthesia machine. A Foregger brand, this was a very expensive top-of-the-line machine in the 1950s. Unfortunately, it gathered dust and was never used! There were two reasons for this: no one knew how to use it, and it utilized water manometers to meter gasses delivered to the patient. If the anesthetist overcorrected the gas flow, water could be expelled from the meters and there would be no way to measure the flow of gases, and in some cases, there would be no flow at all to the patient. Obviously, this could be disastrous for the patient. The flow meters would then have to be recalibrated, a time-consuming procedure that could not be done during surgery.

Without the use of the expensive anesthesia machine, how was anesthesia administered? If possible, procedures would be performed with local anesthesia after heavy sedation with a barbiturate and/or narcotic. In a procedure requiring anesthesia beyond the scope of local anesthesia, the anesthetic was administered with a spinal or regional block. The selection of a general anesthetic was avoided if possible because of the limited equipment and very limited talent for administration. The limited talent was provided by resident psychiatrists on a rotating schedule. These doctors were far removed from clinical medicine and had only very general information about anesthesia techniques. Moreover, nearly all had poor English language communication skills.

An ether induction was a most frightening experience for the whole team when an inept doctor began the procedure! Lacking the use of the anesthesia machine, general anesthesia was administered by the open-drop method using ether or chloroform. The open-drop technique used a wire mesh mask shaped to fit over the mouth and nose. The mesh mask was covered with multiple layers of gauze, and ether was slowly dropped onto the gauze in increasing amounts until the patient lost consciousness and entered the desired depth of anesthesia. Regulating the drip rate altered the depth of anesthesia. During surgery in those days, the head nurse had to step in to guide the doctor, suction the patient, secure the airway, and repeatedly advise the doctor about the anesthetic depth. Maintaining the airway with a special tracheal (endotracheal) tube was never attempted.

This anesthetic technique seemed simplistic and used minimal equipment. Nonetheless, the induction of anesthesia was frequently a harrowing experience for the patient, the untrained physician/anesthetist, and the surgical team. Prior to induction, the patient's arms and legs had to be securely restrained. This tended to set off a wave of fear in the patient, who was not medicated prior to entering the OR. Denying the sedation (premedication) avoided the respiratory depression that accompanied the sedation. This allowed deeper breathing of the irritating, vaporized ether and a more rapid descent into unconsciousness.

As increasing drops of ether were placed on the gauze mask, the pungent, irritating vapor caused breath-holding and extreme efforts by the patient to free himself from the mask. As induction proceeded, the irritating vapor would very often instigate coughing, laryngospasm, and vomiting, thus slowing the induction and exposing the patient to hypoxia and aspiration of gastric fluid. Finally passing through the induction and excitement period, the maintenance of unconsciousness was continued by varying the ether drip rate. The body fat becomes a reservoir for absorbed ether, slowing emergence after surgery. To hasten recovery, the anesthetist would slow ether administration well before the end of the operation, allowing the fat-stored ether to be freed into the blood and exhaled and speeding recovery.

Scrubbing in for a case meant scrubbing the hands to the elbow with PHisoHex soap for five minutes followed by a careful foot-pedal-operated germicidal rinse with Zephiran. Putting on the gown and gloves was a precise procedure to protect the sterility of the gown and to keep the hands clean. Donning the latex gloves after powdering the hands with a starch powder was most difficult. Putting on the gloves was always under the stern, watchful eye of the circulating nurse. Accidentally contaminating a pair of gloves invoked severe criticism because of the labor and time involved in the preparation of the gloves. I solved that potential problem by always selecting a pair of gloves a half size too large for my hands.

Preparing gloves for sterilization was labor intensive. The gloves had to be washed and hung on wooden pegs to dry. When dry, the gloves were placed into a small, windowed box containing fine starch powder. Each glove was handled so that the fingers were inflated somewhat and observed for puffs of powder, which indicated a pinhole leak that could cause later contamination. Finally, the paired, powdered, and sized gloves were placed in a cloth pocket with a packet of starch powder, double-wrapped, and autoclaved.

In the final portion of my first year, I was rotated through the OR for a month. It was an exciting and anxious assignment. Scrubbing in for major surgery usually required two scrub nurses. The second scrub kept the back table with instruments neat and helped the first scrub. The first scrub passed the surgeon instruments and sutures and held retractors as needed. Frequently, at the skin closure, the surgeon would usually drop out and turn over the final suturing to the assistant, and the first scrub would step up to assist.

We would privately practice passing instruments to each other to memorize them and speed the response to the surgeon. We also attempted to get the loudest and most painful snap in the gloved hand. Once developed, this was one of the few ways that the scrub nurse could express anger toward the surgeon. The surgeon frequently took note of it and inquired about the nurse's irritation. Usually it was a response to his misdirected anger, the staining of the mayo stand (instrument stand) with a bloody hand or instrument, or grasping an instrument from the mayo stand without requesting it. A clean, well-organized mayo stand ranked high in the circulating nurse's evaluation.

Praise was not in the circulating nurse's vocabulary. No criticism meant that I did a good job scrubbing, including keeping my mayo stand neat and free of bloodstains. It mattered not that the surgeon had stained the mayo stand. I was supposed to intercept the bloody instrument or bloody hand before it reached the mayo stand.

The range of surgery performed was similar to any community hospital. General surgeons described the procedures as bread-and-butter surgeries, operations frequently performed that helped to put bread and butter on his table, among other niceties. The only unusual procedure performed at the hospital was lobotomy, described previously. Most surgical emergencies at any hour were transferred to Binghamton City Hospital. This reflected the difficulty of securing a surgeon after hours as well as the lack of interest by the attending psychiatrist.

When surgery was to be performed on a woman that required exposing her genitalia, no male students were allowed to scrub or even be in the operating room. This was a reflection of sexual sensitivity in the 1950s. Instead, we would be given instrument cleaning and wrapping assignments.

The usual daily Central Supply duties included filling the eighteen-inch round metal dressing canisters that arrived from the medical floors of the various buildings. These canisters were stocked with a selection of small gauze pads and large abdominal (ABD) pads, roller gauze, and other sterile items that a ward might need. Following sterilization, the canisters were sealed and set aside for the patient trustee from each building to pick up.

An interesting item for sterilization was the P-pad or V-pad. The perineal or vulval pad was a twelve-inch cotton square appropriately folded for placement within underclothes during menstrual flow. The soiled V-pad would be placed into a cloth bag, sent to the laundry, and later delivered to Central Supply. The hospital did not invest funds to purchase ready made, disposable sanitary pads, so Central Supply would sterilize baskets of the pads. I wondered even then about the comparative cost of the washing and sterilizing of the pads versus the factory made, disposable pads.

An assignment to the OR was not all work. A secret benefit was the access to 98 percent absolute ethyl alcohol. The assigned student would be sure to only remove four to six ounces at a time, of course. But that was more than enough for our purposes! We'd gather in a room with glasses in hand and a quart of canned orange juice from the kitchen, and we would add the alcohol. This refreshment made for an evening of vigorous study and discussions.

WARD 6

I enjoyed Ward 6 the most. It was part of a wooden annex connected to the main building. The annex had no separate building identity. It was a two-story structure with an outpatient clinic occupying the first floor. The male and female surgical wards, Wards 5 and 6, were upstairs. The surgical units and Central Supply were between them.

Medical/Surgical Building

Ward 6 contained ten ward beds, a small dayroom, and four private rooms. The private rooms were primarily reserved for employees. I occupied one of those beds when I was admitted with a fever of 103. It was a bad case of the flu, and I needed fluids badly. I was given penicillin intramuscularly, which today is no big deal, but in 1950 penicillin was reconstituted in 10-cc vials containing 50,000 units/cc. The thick, white, oily solution had to be administered through a large twenty-gauge needle that injected it deeply into the buttocks. After the first dose, I dreaded the succeeding doses because the reusable needle was large and usually dull, and the thick penicillin created a painful absorbable pocket deep within my buttocks. Throughout my training, I gave hundreds of those shots and each time I had empathy for the patient. The advent of disposable needles in the late 1950s erased much of the discomfort of injections, as did aqueous preparations of antibiotics.

My first senior assignment to Ward 6 was on the twelve-to-eight shift. The charge nurse was an older man who lived only a few hundred yards away from my home on Colesville Road in 1942. I was never aware that he was an RN. Besides, whoever heard of a male nurse? They were very quiet neighbors, and I knew them very casually. He turned out to be a really sharp nurse and was about five years from retirement.

During this shift, I learned the fine points of passing a Levin tube, which was used to drain fluids and gases from the gastrointestinal tract. A Levin tube is a tube about one-eighth of an inch in diameter. It is inserted through the nose and passed into the stomach. In the 1950s, the tube was rubber and reusable but became limp with many uses. The secret to rapid success was to stiffen the tube by soaking it in ice water, encouraging the patient to drink water during the passage, and using haste in passing the well-lubricated tube while it was still rigid. Otherwise, the tube would become as limp as a wet noodle. With a warm, limp tube, failure was guaranteed. The only solution was to retreat to the supply room to resoak it or to rummage through the drawers for a stiffer tube. The use of a topical anesthetic to ease its passage was unheard of.

The Levin tube was then attached to a Wangensteen suction apparatus that continuously emptied the stomach's contents. The Wangensteen suction apparatus was the only way in the 1950s to apply a predictable, continuous vacuum and avoid harm to the stomach. It involved a two-quart bottle of water that created a vacuum as it flowed into a similar bottle beneath. It used the Venturi principle. The bottles were attached to an axle that allowed manual rotation so that a full bottle was always draining and creating suction. When there was a great deal of drainage or a leak in the connections, the nurse would need to return to the bedside frequently to rotate the bottles.

Ward 6 provided my first and only experience with malarial treatment (pyrotherapy) for tertiary syphilis. In 1950, penicillin was just being explored for treatment of syphilis of the central nervous system. Medical treatment was limited to fever therapy and/or treatment with arsenical compounds. The overall success rate in treating neuralgic syphilis with pyrotherapy is about 33 percent, which is a very good outcome compared to the 3 or 4 percent with the arsenical drugs. Still, a failure rate of 66 percent was indeed depressing.

The treatment involved infecting the patient with malaria, which in a few days produced paroxysms of fever up to 105 degrees approximately every other day. After eight to ten paroxysms of fever, the treatment is terminated with quinine. During these spikes of fever, the patient becomes delirious, restless, and dehydrated from perspiration. All efforts were made to restrain the patient and preserve the IV to cope with the dehydration from perspiration. Maintaining the IV in the arm of a psychotic, restless patient was difficult because the needles used were steel and not the flexible plastic catheters used today. When the course of treatment was finally terminated, the patients were exhausted, frequently anemic, jaundiced, and experiencing multiple oral herpes sores and bruises at every likely spot for IV access. Determining the success of the treatment would be weeks away.

My first, and still the most major preoperative prep, occurred during a night shift when a semicomatose patient was transferred from another building for trephining for a subdural hematoma he developed following a fight with another patient. It fell to me to shave his head completely, first with clippers and then with a double-edged razor. Then I had to scrub his head, remove his clothes, and gown him while the RN started the chart and an IV. It should be noted that in 1950, it was illegal for RNs to start IVs, but at Binghamton State Hospital, that regulation was ignored. I went off duty while the patient was still in the OR but found him alert and in reasonably good spirits the next night.

Another nighttime emergency was a patient admitted with an embolus from an unknown source. It had lodged in his upper arm and was blocking blood supply to the arm. When I encountered him, the patient's lower arm was already becoming cyanotic and mottled and needed immediate intervention. The psychiatrist responsible for the patient attempted a fumbling brachial plexus block in an effort to dilate the vascular tree around the blocked vessel. Considering the doctor's lack of familiarity with the procedure, he did achieve minimal success in restoring circulation to the arm. The patient was transferred to a downtown hospital, and I never learned of the outcome. The odds of salvaging the arm were about fifty-fifty, considering the state of the art in vascular surgery in the 1950s.

I spent a month on Ward 6 and regretted leaving for another ward. The night shift was agreeable, the RN was a good teacher, and I was able to care for physically ill patients who just happened to be psychotic. I was not to return there during my training.

MAIN BUILDING

The main building, "the Castle," contained the administrative offices of the hospital, the hospital manager (administrator), and his assistant. There were also offices of the major department heads and their supporting staff. One of the floors held the electric and insulin shock wards. Occupants of the remainder of the main building were patients in open wards. These wards allowed patients free access to the campus beyond the locked doors.

Assigned to these wards were patients who were psychotic but had control of their special disabilities and were relatively free of interruptions to daily life. They were trustees and worked in the various departments in the hospital. In this group were also long-term patients, free of psychoses and able to be discharged but with no home or family support. These patients, having lived within the hospital's walls for many years, could not cope with daily civilian life. Very little provision was made to assist these patients to adapt to life outside the hospital through a halfway house, so they remained as permanent residents. They provided the extra labor to make the hospital function effectively, which gave them a worthwhile purpose in life.

BARBERS

The barbershop, beauty shop, post office, and some clerical offices were located in the annex that connected Ward 6 to the main building. Employee haircuts cost a dollar. The shop atmosphere easily resembled a barbershop in any small town, with chatter about the news and sports, except the gossip was all about the goings-on on the Hill.

There were about four barbers circulating about the various buildings and giving shaves once a week to those who couldn't shave themselves because they were too busy hallucinating or were disconnected from reality. It was always an interesting experience to observe the shaving process. Patients would line up, and a trustee barber assistant would keep a few patients lathered up as they waited their turns. Some patients didn't understand or misinterpreted the lathering within their psychoses and would continually wipe the lather off, only to have it reapplied until restrained by an attendant. When it came time for the hallucinating or overactive patient to be shaved, he frequently had to be forcefully seated and head restrained. A remarkable thing happened many times when the barber began to apply the straight razor. The patient would suddenly remain still for the five or six strokes of the straight-edge blade and then renew the body movements dictated by the hallucinations. It was as if the knowledge of the danger of the blade broke through the patient's private world and allowed him to remain still for the shave.

I'm sure that a patient must have received a laceration considering the number of shaves given, but I never observed one. These barbers were remarkable in their agility, speed, and skill in laying on the straight razor. By regulation, a special razor guard was supposed to be used, but I never saw it in practice.

OUTPATIENT CLINIC

The outpatient clinic for patients and employees was beneath Ward 6. Here, I was involved in preventive care and treatments for employees and patients and followed up on doctor's orders. This included giving medications, immunizations, and dressing changes and assisting with EKGs and x-ray procedures.

Obtaining an EKG was not the simple thing that it is today, with the custom-made electrodes and immediate computer-generated diagnosis. In the 1950s, after tedious skin cleansing and electrode jelly application, the electrodes were connected to the skin with suction cups or silver plates attached with elastic bands. Each lead of the twelve lead EKG had to be printed on individual strips of sensitive paper. If the calibration of the machine was correct and the stylus had ink, maybe a stable trace would be obtained that had no artifacts. Of course getting a psychotic patient to remain still for the tracing confounded the procedure. Getting a complete EKG required switching manually to each lead and snipping and attaching a strip to a display page. It was not unusual to run four of five feet of strip to get a stable, readable EKG on each lead.

Taking routine x-rays has changed little from the 1950s. Developing x-ray plates has changed significantly. Back then, the x-rays had to be developed similar to a black-and-white photograph, using a dark room, immersing the plates in successive chemical tanks, and finally washing them and drying them. For the x-ray technician and myself, it was a win–win relationship. He had a willing assistant, and I learned a great deal about actual x-ray procedures and even more about developing x-ray plates.

While assigned there, I was able to help the assistant superintendent test patients. He was in his own little world, devoting his time to conducting a psychological test called the Szondi (pronounced with a silent S) test. The Szondi test measured the passiveness versus aggressiveness of the tested subject. At one end of the scale was total passiveness, the ultimate female, and, of course, the opposite end was total aggressiveness, the ultimate male. It measured the subject's sadomasochistic tendencies. In theory, everyone fit somewhere in between, with perfection being in the middle of the scale. He frequently invited employees to participate, I guess to increase his "normal" or control base of tested persons. Taking the test involved quickly choosing persons you were drawn to, repelled by, disliked, or feared from groups of black-and-white pictures. All the photos were well worn and tattered, and none of the pictures was in any way appealing. It was rather like a rogue's gallery of pictures. I took the test and fell to the left of the middle, a somewhat aggressive personality, even though I was assured that I was normal!

DENTAL CLINIC

One dentist and one aide comprised the dental clinic to provide complete dental care for nearly three thousand patients. While many of the patients were uncooperative and would not allow dental procedures, the remainder would easily conform to the dental chair and simple procedures. These patients, if at home and psychiatrically free of symptoms, would probably visit their dentists regularly. Locked in a ward, not encouraged to brush their teeth and in most cases without a toothbrush, their teeth deteriorated rapidly. In addition, an increasingly larger percentage of patients were aging and needed more intense care such as bridge work and dentures. Dental care was essentially not available because of the limited staffing and inadequate funding for dental repairs, so the dentist limited himself to dental emergencies from toothaches to repairing injuries from fights and falls.

NORTH BUILDING

The North building was a two-story custodial building, with four wards, a large entry, and a huge centrally placed dining room/kitchen. Until the late 1930s, the North building was a horse and carriage barn.

North Building

My assignment was Ward 11. The four huge fireplaces in the center of the dayroom, presumably to keep the livestock warm, were the main feature. It was the medical ward for the building and was limited to ambulatory patients with various medical problems. The other three wards were either custodial wards or wards that housed the workers engaged in landscaping or working on the outlying hospital farms at Five-Mile Point.

Two nurses were assigned to the building: the supervisor, Mr. Thomas, and Ward 11's charge nurse, Mr. Miller. Mr. Thomas always had a wad of chewing tobacco distorting his cheek. He was never far from a wastebasket or the spit cup he carried for spitting. I couldn't help but admire his ability to avoid splashing tobacco spit onto his white uniform! When I was assigned to Ward 11, he was more than fifty years old and probably destined to retire from there because of his coarse ways. Mr. Thomas had worked in the ambulance service out of Bellevue Hospital in the days when ambulance calls were answered with a doctor and nurse actually in the ambulance. Mr. Thomas made rounds at the same time each morning, walking rapidly through the ward and ignoring the patients. I was accorded the same lack of recognition.

Mr. Miller, though, was quite different. He was a chatty, narrow-minded, and anxious fellow. His biggest concerns, and never far from the front of conversations, were his complaints about the verbal abuse from his wife and in-laws, who lived with him. In addition, his wife was a free spender, and the court had somehow required him to support his in-laws and take them into his home. Equally vocal were his complaints about the free flow of money out of the bank account. I faulted him for not being man enough to take action to correct his situation.

NORTH BUILDING

Caring for the Ward 11 patients was fun. In addition to the usual passing of medications, it was my responsibility to change the dressings on the few patients with stasis ulcers on their legs resulting from immobility and vascular disease. I became quite adept at generously applying coal tar ointment to the ulcers and wrapping the limb with plain gauze bandage that remained in place all day thanks to my prenursing first-aid training. Today, applying a bandage to a limb with self-adhesive gauze is effortless.

I was able to spend time with patients in the smoking area, which was also the latrine and shower room. Having a smoke with them there gave me an opportunity to establish some rapport and become friends with many of the patients.

Brother Fabian, a monk from a nearby monastery, is one patient I remember well. His Parkinson's disease had progressed so that he developed serious personality changes in addition to the severe tremors. He was a quiet, gentle man who continually prayed his rosary. It was a pleasure to assist him with eating and personal care. Some days, he would become assertive, even assaultive. It didn't help his mental state to be receiving scopolamine three times a day to help control the tremors and salivation. His only visitors were the nearly semiannual visits from the monastery. Within a year after my reassignment, I heard that he passed away quietly on Ward 11.

Another patient stands out in my memory: an elderly schizophrenic and long-time patient at the hospital. He was oriented to his environment and even helpful about the ward while actively hallucinating and conversing with "them." His true love was four-handed pinochle that he played with a single deck. His hallucinations and conversations with the mental voices would continue throughout a game, yet he was amazingly able to expertly play the game. He knew the play of the cards and just about knew which cards each player held halfway through a hand. He was nearly always a winner.

There was a huge, well-muscled, obese black man who spent his entire day in his favorite chair. He got up only to go to the dining room or to bed. All the patients knew to avoid his chair or be ready to face a showdown. The patient was allowed to place his chair in the same location each day, or you could expect a disruption in the ward's peaceful atmosphere. He had one other quirk: he enjoyed being nude and covered himself only with a blanket on cold days! His nudity was tolerated to maintain the ward's peace. This man was well aware of his surroundings though actively hallucinating all day. There were few female visitors to the ward because all visitors were taken to a visiting room in the interior of the building to avoid exposure to this patient and the dismal surroundings.

On the occasion when a female affiliating student would be assigned for the day, the staff would be on guard for this patient's predictable response. His gaze would be fixed on a female student, and he would become obviously aroused because he was nude and sexually very well endowed. He would not allow himself to be covered and would yell at the student to watch him masturbate. An orgasm would soon follow with copious ejaculations. Naturally, the student would be long gone before the climax and would run into the office with a deep flush and intense embarrassment. After the student had departed the ward, we'd have a great laugh while recalling how long the different students stopped and stared at the man's exhibition before exiting. The 1950s was not a sexually liberated decade, and such a sight must have made a deep impression on the young women, as the indignant responses from the nursing office showed. Eventually the female students were no longer assigned to Ward 11.

I would frequently be asked to make rounds on the other wards and the cafeteria during meals. The wards were invariably clean and well-kept as was the cafeteria. The North building's wards were just as dreary as most of the rest of the hospital. I understood that furnishings were kept to a minimum for safety's sake, but I chafed at the poor lighting and the desperate need for painting.

The cafeteria had no windows and lighting so poor that I had difficulty identifying the patients and observing the food. I wondered how the attendants sorted their assigned patients. Mealtimes were invariably peaceful, but the background noise of the clattering metal plates and the noise coming out of the kitchen made conversation difficult. Upon reflection, I should have passed through the dinner line with the patients and experienced their meals to better understand this portion of the patient's daily life.

BELLEVUE: OPENING ANOTHER DOOR

Another facet of my new lifestyle began in September 1951. The time had come to spend a year at Bellevue Hospital to get the necessary medical and surgical training. Binghamton State Hospital couldn't generate enough clinical experience, which required the affiliation at Bellevue.

I really didn't look forward to leaving Binghamton State Hospital because I had come to regard the hospital and my daily life there as a pleasant, secure experience. New York City and Bellevue Hospital were an unknown quantity, a disruption. I was going to Bellevue with nine male classmates, which offered some comfort. My female classmates were to affiliate at Metropolitan Hospital on Welfare Island in the East River as part of the contract with New York State. It was a very isolated place in the largest city in the world and was served by a ferry that only operated about fourteen hours a day.

Mom and Pop drove me to New York where Mom's sister lived, on the lower East Side. The next day, they dropped me off in front of Bellevue. I entered at the employee and ambulance entrance on Twenty-Sixth Street and received directions from a completely unfriendly, disinterested guard. This guy typified the media impression of New Yorkers: rude and uninterested. As I walked, dragging my footlocker the few hundred yards to the emergency room entrance, I was repelled by the collection of dirt and litter. It was enhanced by the crude construction fence along the way. I had to pass a few ambulances in getting to the ER, which was much smaller than I imagined and jammed with people from all walks of life, overflowing to the ambulance dock.

Once past the ER crowd, I entered a wide hallway that seemed to extend forever. It was filled with destination-driven people. I dragged my only luggage, a footlocker, into the elevator of the C&D building, going to the sixth floor, which contained the Mills School of Nursing for Men and rooms for the students. The Mills School of Nursing for Men opened in 1888 as a school to train male nurses to work in men's wards of hospitals. The Mills School of Nursing for Men and Bellevue School of Nursing merged in 1929, becoming the Bellevue Schools of Nursing and even later changing to Hunter-Bellevue School of Nursing.

Getting off the elevator on the sixth floor, I found my way to the front desk and received my assignment to room 616, a room that I was to share with my classmate, Lee. The room was strictly functional: a bed, a dresser, and a bedside table for each of us and a sink. The window provided a view over Twenty-Sixth Street toward the construction of an unknown building. During the first six months of my tour, the sound of pile drivers would reverberate against the building and rattle the windows. Fortunately, the noise only occurred during daytime hours.

My roommate, Lee, was a veteran and had attended a western New York college for a year before entering nursing. It was a fortunate pairing since we had become good friends during the past year at Binghamton State Hospital. My eight other classmates were within shouting distance on the same floor, scattered among nearly sixty Mills students and a dozen more affiliating students from other New York State psychiatric hospitals.

FINDING MY WAY

Since it was Saturday, I was free to take my map of the hospital and explore. I became lost more than once because the hospital was not one building but an alphabet of lettered buildings from A to S. Each lettered portion of a building contained medical specialties. For instance, the A&B building was medicine, the C&D building was thoracic and the Mills School of Nursing, the F&G building was surgery, etc.

Later, I took a walk along the hospital frontage on First Avenue that extended from Twenty-Sixth Street to Thirtieth Street. I didn't stray far because I was afraid I'd get lost. I had a hard time adjusting to the variety of noises assaulting me from vehicles and the shouts of people. As I walked, I would go through zones of foreign odors emanating from food, garbage, and filth everywhere. Of course, the interiors of businesses were clean, but it was obvious that the city was fighting a losing battle with grime and trash. Completing the negative scene were the bums and winos sitting or lying in doorways. Each block held six or eight of these unfortunate people. I wondered if I would ever become used to the cacophony of this seemingly failing society. Yet it wasn't long before I did adjust to it all, even reveling in it. I also discovered that beyond the Lower East Side was an attractive, clean New York City.

ASSIGNMENTS

On Monday morning, all the affiliating students assembled in the nursing school building where the Mills School administration mixed with the Bellevue Hospital School of Nursing, which had only female students. Following the usual orientation and ethics lectures, we were given our ward assignments. The affiliating students were randomly assigned to the various medical services in the A&B building while the Mills students were scattered throughout the hospital. Some of the affiliating students were immediately assigned to the evening and night shifts. I was lucky and drew the day shift.

B6 was my assigned ward. It was populated by male adult patients with medical, nonsurgical diseases. The ward was a wide open ward with a normal census of about forty to fifty patients. The beds were aligned in four rows. Each patient had a metal bedside stand that contained personal toiletries, a roll of toilet paper that also served as facial tissues, a urinal, and a bedpan. When procedures or examinations were required, a screen made with a galvanized pipe frame with a sheet thrown over it was brought to the bedside for patient privacy. This occasional screening was the only patient privacy.

During the winter months, the census would increase by as much as fifty percent with Bowery bums or winos or, in today's parlance, homeless persons. These men suffered the medical problems that accompany cold weather exposure and alcoholism plus other conditions requiring hospital admission. They enjoyed and appreciated the hospital stay, which provided a warm bed, decent meals, and good medical care. The big disadvantage was the inability to satisfy alcohol dependence. Once dried out, though, they relished the ward life and wanted to remain in-house and out of the weather. I couldn't blame them because discharge meant exposure to the miserable New York winter weather and the need to forage for food. When the initial medical admission was cleared, it was common for the patient to search for reasons to extend the admission. The doctors usually were happy to accommodate them so they could be transferred to a different service and off their wards.

Entry into Ward B6 necessitated passing by a rudimentary lab, a small conference room, the patients' bathroom, and the linen room. Passing this area led one to the huge expanse of the ward. On the left, was the nurses' station, which was two desks pushed together and surrounded by a half dozen chairs. On the right were the medication cabinet, dressing cart, and entry into the supply cupboard that held the extra dressings and necessary housekeeping supplies. The forty-plus patient load was cared for by a head nurse, a staff nurse, three or four aides, and an RN ward instructor who monitored the two or three student nurses.

We received our patient assignments following a brief tour of the ward and the reading of the ward rules at 7:00 a.m. Each of us received five patients to completely care for, except for medications and treatments. This meant bed bath, linen change, and all else that was necessary. When I was lucky, a couple of patients would be ambulatory, and I could speed through my assignment. More often, I drew patient assignments that required much more intense care, such as oxygen tent, tracheostomy care, urinary catheter, and Levin tube care. This extra care involved extensive charting that might make me late for class. I inwardly roiled at the difficult assignments, but I now realize that they made me a better nurse.

By midmorning, I was expected to have my morning patient care finished and be ready to attend class. I had great difficulty getting it all completed early in my tour. Even so, I nearly always came to class with my white uniform spotted with unknown chemicals and body fluids that gained criticism from the WI (ward instructor) and the raised eyebrows of the class instructor. Other students had similar problems, and it made me feel a kind of kinship with them.

After about a week, I was moved up to treatments, which I really enjoyed. My assignment to the treatment cart meant that I had to keep it fully stocked and cleaned and assist in the treatments. Unfortunately, I seldom changed dressings of any nature. That was the job of the third-year medical student or the intern. If the dressing change was really involved, the first-year resident took over.

In the 1950s, latex gloves were seldom worn except to attend to draining and infected wounds or when performing a minor surgical procedure. Hand washing was the rule and woe to the one, of whatever rank, who ignored it. Latex gloves were reusable and manufactured in sizes. The hospital's central supply had to wash and test each glove for pinhole leaks using a starch powder in a closed box. The gloves were double-packaged and sterilized in the autoclave. It was an expensive operation that was repeated after each use, so one did not frivolously contaminate gloves. Economical, sterile, and disposable latex gloves didn't become available until the next decade. Today, everyone in patient care wears disposable latex gloves. Unfortunately, the gloves have become a source of contamination and transmission of infections. The gloves are worn unchanged from patient to patient and contaminate equipment that others normally handle without gloves.

Intravenous access, starting infusions, and drawing blood for the lab was, in the 1950s, not a nursing function but was limited to the interns and lower-ranking residents. On a number of occasions, a struggling intern turned the IV access over to me, because drawing blood for the lab and starting IVs was routine ward duty for nurses at Binghamton State even though it was illegal in New York State.

Infusions in the 1950s were a major undertaking. For starters, the needles were steel. At Bellevue, there was no choice of needle style. Most needles were the bayonet style rather than the short bevel that was best for IVs and were reused after sterilization by boiling in the ward sterilizer. A needle was determined to be sufficiently sharp if it did not show an obvious burr and passed through a dressing sponge without catching the material. The IV setup consisted of a glass container with a drip chamber attached to plastic tubing and a needle adapter. This equipment was a pleasant upgrade from Binghamton State Hospital's rubber tubing that was silk-tied to connectors, the drip chamber, and needle adapter.

The most difficult part of starting an infusion was in guiding the needle along the course of the vein. Simply penetrating the vein guaranteed later failure and leakage of fluid into the surrounding tissue. Once in place and securely taped, the arm was secured to a padded splint to prevent disrupting the needle and having to start the infusion again. Ideally, the needle placement avoided a joint so that the arm could be flexed without disruption.

Advancement to passing medications was the premier assignment and an unspoken acknowledgement of the WI's confidence. I was given the narcotics key, which was attached to a wide black ribbon to display prominently around my neck. This clearly identified to everyone that I was the medication nurse and had access to the medication cabinet and narcotics box. It is interesting to recall that Demerol, the favored narcotic at that time, was held in 20-cc vials. The narcotic sheet recorded each dose administered. Because of the tendency to slightly overdraw each dose due to the very slight inaccuracy of the syringes, there was always a shortage of one to five ccs at the emptying of the vial that had to have written acknowledgment by the pharmacy and the charge nurse.

Pouring medications was a generic term for preparing medications to distribute to the patients. The starting point for getting the medications ready was a cart with a tray to support up to forty one-ounce glass medication cups. Each patient had a one-inch by two-inch name card with medication identified. This meant that a patient with multiple medications would have a card for each medication and the administration time listed. On a medical ward, a patient would have multiple medications and a handful of cards to sort. The card would be inserted into a slot behind the medication glass. Medication would be placed into the glass following the "three rule." First, you had to read and confirm the medication for the patient when selecting it. Next, you had to confirm the med again when pouring it, and third, you had to confirm the medication for the patient when returning the bottle to the shelf.

"Passing the meds" involved confirming the patient's name by his wristband, addressing him by name, and checking the correct medication. The medication nurse had little time for any other duties since completion of the first round of medication distribution blended into the next round.

During my assignment to Ward B6, my Uncle Frank, who was married to my Mom's sister, was admitted with coronary heart disease to a lower ward. Before the 1960s, having a coronary (heart attack) meant complete bed rest with minimum physical exertion for two to four weeks, followed by gradual return to activity. Uncle Frank was an aggressive former army sergeant who chaffed at the enforced bed rest. Today he would be described as an alpha male. I liked Uncle Frank, but I barely knew him, and we had little in common. I'm embarrassed to admit that I only visited him a few times while assigned to the A&B building and not at all after assignment to another service. My mental excuse was the pressure of ward work and studies, which I now acknowledge as a lame reason for indifference. Also, during this period, I only visited my Aunt Helen, Frank's wife, a few times, though I had the free time to do so. Looking back, I admit to being self-absorbed, enveloped in the Bellevue experience, and enjoying the big city.

EXPLORING THE HOSPITAL

During my assignment to B6, I also explored the hospital. It may seem like a waste of time, but I enjoyed getting out of the confines of my room and studying in one of the bench seats in the main lobby or in the emergency room. It was a pleasant diversion to study the varieties of people that passed by. The uniqueness of Bellevue was that all classes of people brushed shoulders with each other, from the Bowery bums to the well-dressed upper class.

On another day, I would attempt to get lost by walking through the tunnels that lay beneath and connected the buildings. I always wore my uniform, which was a sort of visual pass to nearly everywhere in the hospital. One of the most interesting places that I stumbled into was the morgue.

When I entered the morgue, I was immediately confronted by an aide and asked to leave, even though I was wearing my uniform. I recalled Pop's adeptness at schmoozing to make a sale to upgrade a pinball machine, sell a punchboard, or calm a tense situation. While servicing a pinball machine or jukebox, Pop would deftly approach the owner and discuss, in a most indirect manner,

BELLEVUE: OPENING ANOTHER DOOR

the profits to be gained in offering an illegal punchboard to customers. It amazed me at how successfully he won over the customers and sold the punchboards. Punchboards were thick cardboard boards containing as many as a hundred sealed holes. Within the sealed holes were tiny fan-folded papers that sometimes contained a wise quote or a winning dollar amount. The businessman was guaranteed a generous profit.

Following the disarming small talk, the aide showed me around the morgue, describing the procedure of processing bodies collected from all over Manhattan. These were mainly bodies that required a legally mandated autopsy or that were unidentified persons. There must have been more than a dozen stainless steel drawers large enough to accommodate the bodies under refrigeration. The aide easily slid out a few drawers to show me the more gruesome bodies, including persons torn apart by a subway train and "floaters" towed from the East River to the Bellevue dock.

From the morgue, I entered the mortuary school operatory. I remember clearly the shock of seeing a row of about six naked corpses on enameled tables. A team of two dressed in surgical scrubs and wearing rubber aprons diligently worked to embalm each of the bodies. It seemed like a scene from an awful horror movie. The instructor was most helpful in describing in detail the embalming procedure, but I was experiencing a sensory overload from the formaldehyde odor that permeated the place so I really didn't absorb the information he gave me.

On another exploratory trip, I discovered the old operating theater that was somewhere in the administration building. The theater, constructed of beautifully crafted walnut wood, was abandoned. It seemed that I had stepped back into the nineteenth century. An elevated tier of seats for doctors and students to observe surgery was located on two sides, creating the well. The old operating table with hand cranks remained in the center of the well with porcelain and painted instrument tables positioned about it. It was empty of instruments but kept in clean condition, as if ready for another patient.

I was rotated every few weeks to another medical service in the hospital, working in all of them except psychiatry and neurology. When I was assigned to the surgery and urology ward, I discovered a different method of sterilization: the formaldehyde cabinet.

Instruments that could not be sterilized by chemicals, soaked, boiled, or autoclaved were placed in a large, sealed glass cabinet after thorough cleaning. A small container of formaldehyde crystals was placed in the cabinet and would evaporate in the sealed cabinet. Sterilization required exposing the instruments to the formaldehyde gas for twenty-four hours. One did not delay retrieving a desired instrument with the open door because of the severe pungency of the formaldehyde gas! I have never seen this sterilization technique used anywhere since.

COLOR TELEVISION

While assigned to surgery, I observed color television for the first time. CBS, NBC, and other television developers were competing for their systems to become the national standard for color broadcasting. In a promotional

BELLEVUE: OPENING ANOTHER DOOR

effort, CBS televised a groundbreaking operation from Bellevue's surgery to the American College of Surgeons meeting in the city. The surgery, a bilateral adrenalectomy or removal of both adrenal glands that sit atop the kidneys, was a major undertaking in 1952. In addition, removal of both adrenal glands required detailed postoperative medical support. History reflects that CBS did not become the standard for color TV, but it was exciting to be among the hospital staff gathering in a conference room to watch the progress of the procedure in a nearby operating room in beautiful color on the seventeen-inch television monitor.

KIDNEY DIALYSIS

Kidney dialysis was being developed at Bellevue, along with other major centers. When rotating through the urology service, I was able to examine an early version of a dialysis machine. The machine and its accessory equipment had taken over a patient room and filled the room, leaving only enough space to walk around. The machine looked like, and was probably the size of, a bathtub. Within the "tub" was a cylinder somewhat smaller than the tub. Clear plastic tubes a quarter of an inch in diameter were wrapped around the cylinder multiple times to completely enclose it.

In operation, the cylinder would be bathed in an electrolyte solution. Blood from the patient's artery would be pumped through the tubing while the cylinder rotated in the electrolyte solution. The blood then returned to the patient's vein. This hours-long procedure would restore nearly proper equilibrium to the blood chemistry but would need to be repeated as often as twice a week.

EENT (EYE, EAR, NOSE, AND THROAT)

Cataract surgery deeply impressed me. The criterion for the surgery required the lens to be nearly opaque, termed ripe, before such a major undertaking was indicated. This is not required for today's cataract surgery. Today, mild cataract development is an indication for surgery, which is a twenty-minute outpatient procedure. In 1952, the procedure took one to two hours with general anesthesia. The cornea would be nearly excised and laid back, and the iris and lens were completely exposed. The cataract (lens) would be removed, and the cornea would be meticulously sutured in place. The cornea had to be precisely returned to its previous position without tension or wrinkles or vision would be distorted. When awakening the patient from endotracheal anesthesia, extreme care had to be exercised to avoid patient coughing. A strong cough could dislodge the contents of the eye, resulting in total blindness. During eye surgery, the surgeon did not wear latex gloves but instead doubled the scrub time. In the 1950s, latex gloves were thick-walled compared to today's mass-produced variety. This thickness interfered with the delicate maneuvers the surgery required.

Returned to his bed, the patient had sandbags placed around his head to help keep his head perfectly immobile. For a couple of days, the head of the bed could not be raised, and the head could not be turned. The patient was discharged in a week and later fitted with glasses with extremely thick lenses to attempt to accommodate the loss of the lens. These glasses held the very thick, so-called Coke-bottle lenses, referring to the thickness of a bottom of a Coca-Cola bottle.

The balconies on an upper floor of one of the EENT wards had to be locked because of frequent suicides. On this ward, among other patients, were the patients who had radical neck surgery for cancer. This procedure caused considerable disfiguration from the loss of neck muscles and underlying tissues and injury to nerves. Occasionally more extensive surgery was required, such as removal of portions of the jaw, tongue, and even removal of the larynx. Patients recovering from this terribly disfiguring surgery, upon examining themselves in a mirror, could become naturally very depressed and occasionally committed suicide by jumping from the ward balcony.

GENITO-URINARY SERVICE (GU)

The GU service occupied two wards made up of a twelve and a twenty-plus bed unit. The smaller ward was reserved for the more acute and immediate postsurgical patients. I worked both wards during my assignment there. My dayshift stint was on the smaller ward that was headed by an old, crusty army nurse. I recall clearly the crude and sometimes painful manner with which she treated the patients. For instance, when a patient needed a routine catheter replacement, she would call the patient to the center of the ward to stand next to the treatment cart. The patient would stand with legs widespread and gown pulled behind him. The charge nurse would release the water-filled balloon that retained the catheter in the bladder and remove the catheter. That would occasionally require a sharp, painful tug. With an application of KY jelly, a fresh catheter would be inserted while the patient squirmed, cursed, and backed away. They finally remained still after a scolding and a little cursing by the charge nurse. Catheters were double and sometimes triple the usual catheter size routinely used. At completion, the catheter tip would simply be placed in the bottle that hung from his neck for drainage, and the patient was sent back to his bed.

The GU patient could easily be identified by a length of gauze bandage wrapped around his neck and tied to the drainage bottle that held the catheter tip loosely placed inside. These open-top glass bottles varied from an eight-ounce urine sample size to a quart milk bottle. An array of the sterilized bottles was always in the supply room. The same sort of collection system was used at the patient's bedside. A sterile, sealed, plastic urine drainage bag that prevented ascending infection was still a thing of the future. When a catheter was removed, it would be placed in a water-filled basin in the cleanup sink to be collected later in the day and taken to Central Supply. The catheters would be scrubbed, tested, and resterilized for the next patient. It was unheard of to dispose of a functioning catheter after one use, as is done today. With today's mass production, sterilization, and packaging, it is cheaper and safer to use the single-use disposable catheter. However, this money-saving concept of using disposables has done surprisingly little to decrease ascending infections.

OUTPATIENT CLINIC

I was also rotated through the GU outpatient clinic, the area for treatment of ER referrals and general follow-up care after discharge. It was an enjoyable assignment, with little to do beyond making conversation, assisting with dressing changes, and collecting vital signs. An exception was the assignment to carry out urethral sounding, which gave me the opportunity to do something more advanced than just routine tasks.

Urethral sounding is something that most men would avoid at all cost. Dilatation sometimes becomes a necessary procedure to ensure a clear passage of urine due to an obstructive scarring, most frequently related to complications from gonorrhea. In 1950, there was no satisfactory way to clear the urethra of obstructive scar tissue (strictures), so dilatation or sounding became necessary when urine passage became difficult. It involved inserting a solid stainless steel metal rod, called a sound. It was about ten inches in length and had a gentle L-shaped curve at its end. Sounds are available in multiple sizes, from smaller than a pencil to larger than one's thumb.

The only patients who came to me were the patients who had received soundings multiple times. I was surprised at how many of these men regarded the sounding as a routine matter and could carry on conversation during the passage of the sounds. Fortunately, new admissions for urinary obstruction and those with a history of difficult soundings were not sent to me.

A patient would enter the treatment room with the doctor's note to pass a sound up to a certain size. With the patient lying on the treatment table, the penis would be washed with pHisoHex and draped with sterile towels, and I would then proceed to select a very small sound to initially pass along the urethra into the bladder.

The initial lubricated sound would be nearly the diameter of a pencil. It would be inserted and gently rotated upon reaching the base of the penis, and the tip entered the bladder. The sound would then be removed and a larger size inserted until the prescribed size was reached. The key word in successful treatment was gentle. Using force in passage could easily result in urethral damage or rupture of the bladder.

Another interesting, though distasteful, assignment was prostatic massage. The job was given to male students probably because the residents felt themselves to be a level above the assignment while the female nurses would be excused for sensitivity reasons. The purpose was to collect a sample of spermatic fluid on a microscope slide that was expressed during prostatic massage to send to the lab to examine for gonorrhea's Neisseria bacteria and other organisms. Following the slide collection, we were instructed to extract the maximum fluid with the massage and discard it.

In the treatment room, the patient lowered his pants and bent over a low exam table. I would roll on a "finger cot," a sort of condom that was finger size; lubricate the finger; and insert it into the rectum. The gland was easily reached and was identified by its softness and margins. Within a few moments of massaging the gland, spermatic fluid would begin emerging from the tip of the penis, and a sample was collected on the microscope slide. The slide would be put aside and massage continued until maximum fluid drained from the penis onto a paper towel. During the massage, it was required to determine the size of the gland through manipulations, note any unusual firmness and nodules, and chart the findings.

During my few days assigned to the prostatic massage, I realized that most men found the procedure distasteful. However, the charts reflected that a number of men were returning frequently for the massage and seemed to enjoy the procedure. I resented that I might be giving these men sexual pleasure though I knew that, for many of them, their lives contained few pleasures. While it was distasteful having to deal with male genitalia, being given an advanced procedure to perform was satisfying.

TIME OFF

Later in the year, when the summer sun heated the room, I'd spend a little while in the open window just watching the construction activity on the nearby building and observing the ambulances and people passing by.

While surveying the view, I happened to take notice of activity in an open window in the building that used to be the Mills School. It had been converted to a residence for female aides. From my high vantage point, the open window was positioned where I could clearly see into some of the rooms. I saw an aide disrobe completely and lie on the bed in the hot room that didn't have air conditioning. Naturally, observation of this room became a regular afternoon diversion and a pleasant break from studies!

My days off were staggered to accommodate the ward's scheduling, so having time off with classmates was irregular. I found myself frequently alone, wandering Manhattan for entertainment. Searching the city for entertainment might sound strange, but much of New York's entertainment requires cash. A budget of thirty dollars a month didn't allow for fun times. I discovered Third Avenue and the subway to be a fascinating way to spend the day.

I could spend all day walking both sides of lower Third Avenue, ignoring the thundering noise of the elevated subway. Just browsing at all the junk and stuff in the swap shops (pawn shops) was great entertainment. If I had had the cash, I probably would have filled my room with "treasures," junk collector that I am! If a week passed since my last visit, the Avenue would appear wholly different because of changes in inventory.

The subway was the best adventure. A dime would get me a ride to what seemed like a foreign country. Emerging after as little as a fifteen-minute ride would reveal a different New York with different architecture and a different mixture of odors. Even the pedestrians would have a subtly different attitude.

On the days when I had time to explore New York, I would pore over the *Times* and *New Yorker Magazine* in the library to see what free events were available. To get to a free event meant planning the trip via the subway or bus and walking. The adventure that would cost less than a dollar, including my meal of a Nedick's hot dog and orange juice. Lacking events to attend, I could always fall back on visiting the swap shops and just plain people watching.

BAR HANGOUTS

Two favorite hangouts were Walsh's and Trix's bars. Walsh's was located on the corner of First Avenue and Twenty-Fifth Street. It was a modern tavern that offered very good food at moderate prices and a friendly bar. Off-duty classmates would go there for a few beers and talk. It helped that every third beer was on the house and that the bartenders were mostly friendly.

There was one occasion, however, when a new bartender refused to serve a black guy in our group. He was a Mills student and good friend. When Jim was refused a drink, our group of four raised our voices in objection loud enough that all the patrons in the place could easily hear. Then we announced loudly that we were leaving, would tell all the students at Bellevue about the discrimination, and would ask the students to boycott the place. The manager arrived and quickly pacified us, and we never had a problem again.

Trix's bar, on the other hand, was the opposite in appearance. It was around the corner from Walsh's on Twenty-Fifth Street. The entry was grimy, as was the dark, poorly lit interior. The painted wood booths were showing their age. However, the beer was ten cents a glass—a third less than Walsh's was!

Trix's had become, for many years, the gathering place for Bellevue and Mills students. It was a place where, with the cheap beer, we could be as loud as we wished and even dance a bit. Trix's specialty was the meatball sandwich, both priced cheaply and delicious. But it did lose favor when one in our group was served a sandwich into which a cockroach had found its way. From that day, we all drank the beer and went elsewhere for food. Never mind that the beer glasses might be dirty!

A third bar was called the Garden. It was located on Third Avenue, just a couple of blocks from Bellevue. It was a small insert into the array of commercial businesses. It was another of the poorly maintained bars in Manhattan, but it had a uniqueness that appealed to many of us. The bar had a back room with wood booths arranged in a U-shape that allowed for a small dance floor. Each booth was separated by a trellis that granted a measure of privacy, hence the only indication of a garden. And the booth area was very dimly lit, with a candle at each booth. It was a bar where couples could have very private moments together, and the waitress was discreet. The Garden was the only cheap place nearby where an economically challenged couple could go to complete a romantic date.

HORN & HARDART

When I was flush with cash, I would visit the Horn & Hardart automat. The automat was a wonderful place, where, with a handful of coins, a guy could get a whole meal item by item or just a piece of pie and delicious coffee by inserting the proper coins, opening a windowed door, and removing food.

I had pleasant childhood memories of the automat the couple of times Mom and Pop took us to the city. A visit to the automat was mandatory. Mom and Pop were thrilled with the convenience and having the ready-to-eat food displayed behind tiny windows. Mom just could not resist departing with a souvenir knife, fork, and spoon that carried the heavy stainless steel Horn & Hardart name. These utensils were not like today's plastic throwaways. Horn & Hardart automats have been closed for many years, but a wall with the dispensing doors rests in the Smithsonian Institute in Washington.

GOING HOME

Returning to Binghamton to visit Mom and Pop was only possible a few times during the year due to lack of money for the train fare. Going home required a subway ride to Hoboken to get the iconic Phoebe Snow and a three-hour-plus train ride.

On two occasions, I went to the Bowery and donated blood for five dollars to add cash to the trip home. The actual donation was simple, but the procedure and environment left a great deal to be desired. The donation site was operated by New York University in a slum area in a former business location. In order to enter, I had to wind my way past a crowd of men milling about to get to the registration desk. The form was filled out by a disinterested clerk with an angry attitude. Very minimal questions were asked since it was expected that the donors would be less than truthful.

Following the registration process, I entered a line of men waiting for a finger stick for a drop of blood. The rate of descent of that drop of blood in a copper sulfate solution gave an indication of the hemoglobin level. A descent too slow was an indication of anemia and a cause for rejection. Many of these men would attempt to donate as often as possible to finance their lifestyles, though that only predisposed them to anemia.

Next, I was led into a room with possibly twenty other men and formed into a large circle around a doctor in a dirty lab coat. The doctor said that this was going to be a "short arm" inspection, a term that I had never heard before. We were told to lower our pants and underwear and lift our penises so the doctor could examine them. If uncircumcised, one had to withdraw the foreskin completely for observation of the glans. I didn't see anyone rejected for a symptom of syphilis—a chancre.

Passing the blood drop and penile tests, the time arrived for the blood donation. The skin prep was basic: strong iodine solution followed by a rinse of alcohol. The needle was a sixteen-gauge that looked as big as a pipe attached to plastic tubing that led to an inverted blood bottle containing an anticoagulant. Thanks to the large-bore needle, the donation was over quickly.

With no time for recovery or adjustment, I was directed to a "refreshment" area, where I was offered either a cup of coffee or a shot of unknown whiskey. Though it was early morning, I was among the few choosing coffee. I received my five dollars and was shown the exit. I was told that the blood was numbered and blood type assigned in the blood bank's lab, and it was ready for administration. Who knows how many diseases were transmitted with blood donated in this manner.

I donated blood for cash in New York only two times because it was the most demeaning experience that I had ever had. While I had great sympathy for those men and their level of existence, I resented being exposed to the intense body odors, herded like an animal, and required to display my genitals in such a group fashion.

NEW YORK ATHLETIC CLUB

While walking through a park next to the East River, I stopped to observe a track-and-field team training. Conversation with a coach resulted in a referral to a coach at the New York Athletic Club (NYAC) to try out for their wrestling team. On my next day off, I visited the club on Fifty-Seventh Street, overlooking Central Park.

Upon presenting the track coach's name, I was escorted to meet the wrestling coach. After a pleasant interview and a tour of the huge gym and track, I was invited to train with the team and, if I showed promise, possibly join the wrestling team. It was exhilarating to be allowed into the club, albeit through a side entrance. Training with the club wrestlers and holding my own made me proud. But my hospital schedule made full participation difficult, and I had to withdraw after a couple of months. To be allowed a provisional, limited membership into the NYAC and to practice with upper-level wrestlers remains a special memory. I'll never know if I would have made the team, though I doubt it. The team members were nationally ranked wrestlers.

LEE'S WEDDING

In May, my roommate, Lee, made the decision to get married to Beverly, a classmate who was affiliating at Metropolitan Hospital with our other female classmates.

Lee prevailed on me to make the arrangements as cheaply as possible. The requirements were a church wedding, any denomination was all right, and a sit-down meal for about eight guests at a nice restaurant.

I accepted the task with unusual vigor. After visiting six Protestant churches, I found a pastor at a large Unitarian church, somewhere near Fourteenth Street, who would perform the ceremony in the main portion of the church. The cost of the private ceremony was not an issue, since the pastor was aware that the bride and groom were students and that the marriage was somewhat urgent.

Finding the nice restaurant was an even bigger task. I had to find a restaurant in Manhattan that was economical, and the dinner had to be in a private dining area and be scheduled on the wedding day that was within the pastor's calendar and Lee and his bride's time off. In addition, the preferred meal had to revolve around beef. I finally found a restaurant on the Upper East Side around Fifty-Fourth Street. A midweek wedding in the afternoon was the only possibility, so a private dining room was unnecessary. The sympathetic restaurant manager, aware of the limited resources, provided our party with a fine filet mignon meal with a delicious house wine. It was a fine wedding that proceeded with unusual ease to everyone's satisfaction. The bride and groom had two days off for a honeymoon before returning to duty in separate hospitals.

In two months, Lee asked me for another favor: to help him find an apartment. The requirements were that it had to be cheap and within walking distance to Bellevue. I accomplished the seemingly impossible task after walking the streets near Bellevue. I found a two-room basement apartment consisting of a living room/bedroom and kitchen. As a sort of reward for arranging the wedding and finding the apartment, Lee and Bev invited me to share their first big meal. The Spanish rice was perfectly prepared, but it was so spicy that Lee and I had to force ourselves to eat it and still gush with compliments!

NEW YEAR'S EVE

Uncle Frank and Aunt Helen invited me to a New Year's Eve party at a private club. With no other plans and no money to celebrate, I gladly accepted. It was late afternoon when I joined Uncle Frank and another couple at his apartment on Twelfth Street before we took a subway to the Brooklyn club. I had never heard of the private club and cannot now remember its name, which tells you a great deal about the evening! The second-floor party site was filled with couples already dancing, drinking, and just having a good time. Uncle Frank had apparently recovered well from the heart attack in September and was in a very loud, outgoing mood and in a mood to celebrate in a big way!

Uncle Frank bought rounds of beer and bourbon and insisted that we all drink heavily with him to welcome the entrance of the New Year. Bourbon was not my favorite drink, and I shuddered with each sip. I was a beer drinker, and the booze hit me hard. I dimly remember looking at my watch and reading eleven o'clock, when I excused myself to visit the bathroom. My next memory was stepping off a bus in front of the hospital and finding my way to my room. I have no memory of leaving the club and finding my way back to the hospital. I have only my spiritual guide to thank for my safe return.

I awakened midmorning to a huge hangover that I still recall. I dressed and left the hospital for fresh air and a cup of coffee. While walking north on First Avenue to the far end of Bellevue, I passed a busy Mobile Oil gas station that had only three pumps and a three-bay service area. For reasons beyond logic, I entered the station and applied for a part-time job. The owner of Larry's Mobile was there and gave me an evening job, agreeing to work around my schedule. When I left the station, the awful hangover was nearly forgotten.

LARRY'S GAS STATION

I had only one function at the station, to pump gas. Being a pump jockey is usually an easy job but not at Larry's. Larry's business success depended on the independent taxi drivers. There were few gas stations in Lower Manhattan and a station that catered to the independents was guaranteed success only if the service was fast. A long wait for a fill-up meant loss of income for the drivers. I was kept hustling, pumping gas, checking oil, and washing windows during my whole shift. If a driver felt that I wasn't hurrying, I would feel his curses rain down on me, so I had to appear to hurry faster and smile while feeling his anger.

There were two mechanics to offer major service for the taxis, Checker and Desoto brands, the only models allowed by regulation to ply New York streets. This made service easy and fast. For instance, clutches and brakes were probably the most common repair, and Larry's kept a stock of them on the shelves. The taxi drivers were thrilled at the speed of repairs, as reflected in the mechanics' tips and the repeat business generated. Every taxi carried a large medallion attached to the hood that provided the legal authority to operate. There were a very limited number of medallions issued. A medallion was not transferable without entering a bureaucratic jungle so if his cab was out for service and off the street, he received no income from fares.

By late spring, I was promoted to spend my part-time evening hours at another station that Larry owned in the Bowery. It was a corner station with six pumps, and my only function was to pump gas. There were no other employees there, so I guess that I was the nominal station manager. There were few customers in the late evening hours in this business section of the Bowery, so I could study while working.

Most evenings, the Bowery bums (derelicts) would stop in and ask permission to add water to dilute their gallon jugs of cheap wine, referred to as Sneaky Pete. It was enjoyable to talk with these men, many of them well-educated and with pleasant stories to tell. It was sad to observe the depths to which they had fallen, and I deliberately never explored the reasons for their crashes. I felt blessed at having a job, being in school, and having some extra cash in my pocket, making me a soft touch for these bums. Parting with a dollar (a ten-dollar equivalent today) was easy to do. It helped the man in an unknown way and gave me selfish satisfaction of knowing I helped the unfortunate.

In time, it became more difficult to shift ward assignments to accommodate my work at Larry's station, and I regretfully resigned. I enjoyed the contact with a different stratum of people that the job gave me and secretly felt that I could enjoy working full time at the station.

RINGLING BROTHERS CIRCUS

The Ringling Brothers Circus performed for the patients each year behind the hospital in the large parking area that overlooked the East River. It was an exciting event for everyone, patients, employees and media, and great public relations for the circus that led up to their traditional engagement at Madison Square Garden.

The appearance of the circus was especially exciting considering there was little diversion in the hospital. There was no television, and the only escape from hospital boredom was an AM radio, if one could afford it and find an electrical outlet near the bed. Portable radios were expensive and used equally expensive batteries that could not be recharged.

Each floor of the older buildings had outdoor balconies, and on performance day, the balconies were jammed. At ground level, a sea of patients in beds, in wheelchairs, and on crutches mixed with the ambulatory patients and employees to see the two-hour circus performance.

CLOSING THE CURTAIN ON BELLEVUE

With September approaching, my year at Bellevue was coming to a close. I really didn't want to return to Binghamton and the state hospital. I had grown comfortable with the noise, hubbub, rudeness, dirt, and rotten smell of the Big Apple. While I could only sample a tiny portion of the city's offerings, I wanted to remain and take a bigger bite of that Apple.

With those unsettling feelings, I arranged for Railway Express to ship my footlocker, and I turned my back on New York City.

I found the city increasingly foreign with each return in the following years, proving again that a special period can only be reproduced in memory.

SENIOR YEAR

Returning from Bellevue meant the start of my vacation but not a period to have fun and relax. Following my required physical, I was informed that I had to have major dental work done or drop out of the program.

The need for substantial dental work was not obvious to the casual observer, who would only notice intact incisors. The remainder of my teeth, the few that remained, were so deteriorated that a few were below the gum line. My desire to remain in nursing was the impetus to get the dental work done that I knew I would have to face eventually.

The vacation started with a visit to a dentist who informed me that my teeth were beyond repair and that I needed a full mouth extraction with complete upper and lower dentures. He offered to extract the teeth under anesthesia. I agreed and accepted his referral to an older general dentist who limited his practice to dentures. The plan was to schedule my dental surgery with immediate insertion of dentures. This was a departure from the usual routine of delaying dentures until after full healing. This theoretically limited swelling, reduced pain, and gave the patient an early opportunity to adjust to them. This different plan would allow me time to somewhat heal and return to classes with a normal appearance and be able to communicate.

On extraction day, my old buddy Ron drove me to the dentist's office, where I presented myself and tried rather unsuccessfully to display an aura of confidence. I can recall a poor attempt to start an IV before unconsciousness descended like a window shade.

My next recollection was exiting the office with Ron supporting me. I had a mouth full of bloody gauze. While I was unconscious, the dentist apparently injected a local anesthetic for pain relief during and after the procedure and to also slow bleeding by vasoconstriction of the torn vessels. Pain-free, with a mouth full of cotton gauze and still recovering from the anesthetic while en route to get fitted for my dentures, I was giddy and not fully aware of the magnitude of what just had transpired. Inserting the dentures after minor adjustments was routine. However, my mouth was numb from the local anesthetic, I was drooling bloody saliva, and I had the upper and lower plate in place so I was dismayed by the huge mouthful of foreign material in my mouth. Ron delivered me home to Liberty Street, where I fell into bed and slept until my mother came home from work. I felt that I was awakening from a bad dream until I saw the bloodstained pillow, felt the immense pain, and was unable to talk with the dentures filling my mouth. The pain and oozing slowly diminished in the following days, and I returned to duty with a minimum of discomfort and was able to eat a soft diet that the school office specially arranged for me.

My classmates were considerate of my limited desire to socialize, and as I gradually became adjusted to the dentures, life returned to normal, though I was self-conscious about my appearance. While learning to live with the dentures, I returned to class with a resolve to become a better student.

When I reported to Ward 63 in Fairmont, I was full of state-of-the-art knowledge and cockiness that most fellow students felt after a year at Bellevue. The head nurse was aware of this attitude of returning students. In an effort to deflate my presumed inflated ego, he assigned me to prepare a patient for pickup, who had died during the night. Assigned to help me was an affiliating student from Arnot-Ogden Hospital in Elmira. This student left me breathless at first sight. Joan—beautiful and perfectly groomed in her starched bib and apron—had a smile that could tame a wild animal and eyes so large and brown that they reminded me of a Jersey cow. I fell in love at that moment. Gone was my determination to focus solely on my studies.

It may seem strange to say that preparing the body for the funeral home was a pleasure. We completed the assignment and together tied the ID tag on the patient's toe. I entered into a love affair with Joan that would last the next forty-nine years.

Practically all my free time was spent with Joan for the remainder of her State Hospital affiliation. I was lost in those big brown eyes and hung onto her every word. We discovered that we were psychically close, enjoying the same games, dancing, and even political and esoteric subjects. I never would have believed that I could love someone so intensely in just a few short weeks.

Before Joan's affiliation ended, I traveled to Elmira for the obligatory meeting with her parents, John and Pearl. Joan's parents fit easily into an upper-middle-class income level and style of living. Their home on Cleveland Avenue was perfectly maintained, with a garage for one of their two cars and nearly an acre of land. I could not ignore the custom-built BBQ and the small playhouse built for Joan when she was small. Entering into their two-story frame home presented me with the stark differences between this home and my own on Liberty Street in Binghamton. Everywhere I looked I saw expensive furnishings and antiques that were perfectly coordinated. The living room furniture blended with the wall-to-wall carpeting, adding a large measure of class. Wall-to-wall carpeting was something unheard of in my social sphere. We simply rolled up our carpet and took it with us whenever we moved.

Pearl was most gracious in welcoming me into her home and was full of general chatter, especially inquiries about my family and background. I was deliberately evasive because the Higgins family had no auspicious background. We were just plain folks struggling to make daily life pleasant. My Mom and Pop were experiencing economic hardships similar to their experience in the 1930s, and their home reflected it.

John, on the other hand, was a big, bald Italian. He had little to say to me beyond a quick hello accompanied by a weak, dead-fish handshake and little eye contact. Finished with the amenities, he turned and proceeded to the refrigerator to retrieve a quart of beer and settled into his special recliner. As if on cue, the dinner was ready in the eat-in kitchen when the beer was finished. It was spaghetti, and John piled it high on his plate, smothering the sauce with crushed hot pepper. Following this impressive meal, during which John ignored me and had little to say to Joan or her mother, he abruptly left the table, returned to his recliner to read the paper, and fell asleep. This first weekend introduction was a portent of my future in-law relationship. It was a relationship in which Pearl accepted me into her world but would persistently offer advice and suggestions, and John would consistently ignore me. I never learned the reason for his apparent dislike for me. It could easily have been my less-than-masculine occupational choice, my Irish background, my low economic promise for his daughter, or probably all three.

With Joan's return to nursing school in Elmira, sixty miles distant, I became immersed in studies but traveled to be with her at every opportunity. The hour's drive in my newly acquired 1937 LaSalle club coupe was an adventure because the V8 engine had burnt valves and leaky pistons. The engine was so worn out that I had to keep it running or park on a hill. Starting the car meant putting the gearshift in neutral, removing the wheel blocks, and pushing the car to get it rolling down the hill! Coasting at a reasonable speed, I'd engage the transmission, and the engine would turn over fast enough to start. These short, adventurous separations from Joan only intensified my attraction to her. Within a few months, I'd scrounged enough money for an engagement ring and proposed to Joan. Her acceptance became a supreme event, a marker in my life.

As a senior, my assignments were directed more toward psychiatric nursing than bedside nursing. I had assignments to ambulatory wards in Broadmoor, Fairmont, and the Main Building.

Assignment to the Main Building was an intense, interesting period because I was involved again with the insulin shock/electric shock ward. While assigned to this ward, I realized that I wanted the more intense activity that an advanced specialty, such as nurse anesthesia provided. Psychiatric nursing provided long-term professional satisfactions, but the anesthesia field would provide immediate personal feedback and was more suited to my personality.

The head nurse may have sensed this and assigned me to the electric shock team. Assigned to lead the team on ECT morning under the watchful eye of the head nurse, I stood at the head of the stretcher. It was my duty to adjust the ECT machine's settings because each patient had different convulsive thresholds. It was essential to initiate treatment as quickly as possible as a delay could provoke an aggressive resistance. In addition, I felt personal pressure to minimize the heightened psychological tension that the patient must have felt.

SENIOR YEAR

I became quite adept at applying the conductive jelly to the temples and the latex band around the head that already had the silver disks and wires attached. Once the bite block was inserted into the patient's mouth and I was assured that the team was positioned on each side of the patient to support each limb at the onset of the convulsion, I'd quickly check the machine settings and look to the doctor for the nod to proceed. Following the tonic (rigid) and the subsequent clonic (jerking) of the convulsion, I'd disconnect the electrodes, wipe the jelly from the patient's forehead, and utter a mental prayer that the patient would immediately resume breathing. A small number of patients were slow to resume breathing. They would become mildly cyanotic, at which point the epigastrum was vigorously tapped in hopes that somehow the stimulus of the diaphragm would institute breathing. If unsuccessful, cyanosis deepened and chest compressions would be started. To my relief, all patients finally resumed breathing. I wonder now at how much cerebral damage was caused by hypoxia during the periods of apnea.

With the end of my senior year approaching, Joan and I set a tentative wedding date. First, we had to obtain permission from our school's administration to marry prior to graduation. Entering marriage without permission would mean immediate dismissal for each of us, no matter that we were in the final few weeks of training. While in Elmira, we cemented the date as August 8 if the date was agreeable to my folks. Mom and Pop were enthusiastic about an August 8 wedding because the date coincided with their anniversary. I chose not to reveal that the selection was a complete accident, because their anniversary was far from my mind. However, I enjoyed the unconscious compliment paid to them.

Mom and Pop were beginning to emerge from their economic slump, and Pop helped me to search for and buy a car on credit. The final choice was a beautiful blue 1947 Super Deluxe model Plymouth. It was an automotive leap into the future from the Model A Ford to the modernistic Plymouth. The car had only one defect difficult to solve: the headlights. After a variable time, the circuit breaker would open and the headlights would go out. Driving at night meant always being aware of quick places to pull over and wait for the circuit breaker to automatically reset. Driving the sixty miles to Elmira after dark to be with Joan became an exciting experience!

Preparations for the wedding became progressively more urgent in Elmira, an hour's drive away, while I was blithely going about my daily routine. My future mother-in-law and Joan were immersed in all the wedding details. All I had to do was essentially show up at the altar. I awoke on my wedding day with an overpowering hangover from the bachelor party at Joan's grandparents' home. All I wanted was aspirin and more sleep. Getting married was the last thing on my mind! But thanks to my brother and best man, I arrived well-groomed in my tuxedo and on time for the big day. Later, Joan told me that she wouldn't exit the car at church until she saw me arrive.

August 8, 1953, the day that changed my life, is a collage of memories with none of them clearly embedded in my mind. I definitely recall during the photography session on the church lawn that my new father-in-law shook my hand with little enthusiasm and grimly said, "Well, I guess you'll be taking her to live on a pig farm now." That comment aptly described John's attitude for the next forty-eight years. During those years, we exchanged no more than terse greetings when we met. It was very ironic that a half century later, after the passing of my beloved Joan and the abandonment by his son Ron, I was left to care for John to finally fulfill a promise I made to Joan to look after her parents.

Our best wedding gift was a free week at a cottage owned by Joan's uncle on Lake Lamoka, a two-hour drive away. It was a beautiful little cottage on the edge of the lake with an outhouse as the only disadvantage. We even had access to an oversized rowboat with an outboard motor. The isolation of the cottage offered us the opportunity to really bond together. The honeymoon put to rest every groom's big fear of running out of things to say after a few days.

It was difficult for Joan and me to return to our home schools to wind up our studies and graduate eighteen days later on August 26. Fate seemed to play a prank on us when our schools scheduled graduation on the same day in August and at the same hour. Immediately after graduation, I hurried to join Joan in Elmira, bypassing the graduation party.

Within a week, Joan and I were settled in an apartment on Gerard Avenue. Joan began work at Lourdes Hospital, and I received an assignment to the North building at the state hospital.

REFLECTIONS

Returning to the unkempt hospital grounds today, I'm assaulted with the disappearance of most of the older patient buildings, except for the locked doors of Wagner Hall and Broadmoor. They present a ghostly appearance of peeling paint, tall weeds, trees emerging from the walks, and glassless boarded windows.

It does give me great pleasure to know that modern medicine and patient care have made great progress, resulting in the emptying and abandonment of those buildings. Still, nostalgic memories of sixty years past cascade in my memory.

More than a half century ago, I entered the Binghamton State Hospital nursing program as an immature eighteen year old and, in three years, emerged as a Registered Nurse and a much more mature and considerate person. During this time, I met my future bride and experienced forty-eight wonderful years of marriage. I received an advanced education that, considering my economic status, would not otherwise have been possible. I gained a foundation to proceed to nursing anesthesiology training. I experienced the vacuum of mental health care that existed prior to antipsychotic medications.

One cannot help but reflect on the what-ifs and could-haves of those years. Yet, it is impossible to guess what I would have experienced had I taken a different road in life. I have stumbled on the rocks and ruts along that road, but overall I would not have made any detours. I am satisfied and pleased when I reflect on that journey taken those many years ago.

Binghamton State Hospital, aerial view